"Fascinating, thirst-provoking, and a lot of 'I never knew that about Colorado beer and breweries,' Brewed at Altitude *is a looking glassful of our state history."*

—Charlie Papazian, author of The Complete Joy of Homebrewing *and Founder/Past President, Brewers Association, American Homebrewers Association, Great American Beer Festival and the World Beer Cup®*

"A master class on Colorado beer history. Pop it open and imbibe!"

—Dr. Peter Kopp, author of Hoptopia

"This isn't just a book about beer. It's a book about us. Bonus—you have permission to enjoy a cold brew while reading!"

—Karen Hertz, Chief Brewista and Founder, Holidaily Brewing Company

BREWED at ALTITUDE

• A Beer Lover's History of Colorado •

SAM BOCK & JASON L. HANSON

Foreword by Tom "Dr. Colorado" Noel

Published by American Palate
A division of The History Press
An imprint of Arcadia Publishing
Charleston, SC
www.historypress.com

First published 2025

Manufactured in the United States

ISBN 9781467159098

Library of Congress Control Number: 2025931113

CONTENTS

FOREWORD

Beer has long been America's favorite beverage. But the modern, explosive growth of brewpubs and craft breweries has brought back the neighborhood breweries that characterized pre-Prohibition America. Since 1858, breweries and bars in Colorado have been much more than just a place to drink. Denver's Apollo Hall serves as an example.

Two months after opening as a beer hall, this two-story Larimer Street anchor became a hotel. The next month, in September 1859, the Apollo staged a grand opening ball offering five-dollar dinners, billiards, dancing, and even bedding, all "to the best music available." This drinking, billiards, sleeping, dining, music, and dance hall became Denver's first theater in October 1859, when miners' candlesticks were stuck into the walls and crude benches were set up in the second story. Apollo Hall also accommodated still-churchless Presbyterians, who met there in 1860 despite crashing billiard balls, drunken commotion, and occasional gunfire from the bar below. When the hubbub grew unbearable, ministers led their flocks in the temperance hymn:

There's a spirit above and a spirit below,
The Spirit of love and the spirit of woe,
The Spirit above is the spirit divine,
The spirit below is the spirit of wine.

The zenith of the Apollo's life came in September 1860, when townsfolk gathered there to draft a municipal constitution establishing the "People's Government of the City of Denver." That beer hall experiment in self-governance has evolved into today's City and County of Denver.

I flirted with beer in my books *The City and the Saloon: Denver, 1858–1916* and *Colorado: A Liquid History & Tavern Guide to the Highest State*, but historians Sam Bock and Jason L. Hanson have produced a fuller account focused on the social and economic history of beer. This diligent duo earlier co-produced a superb, major exhibition about beer for History Colorado. It, and this book, put beer into the broader context of the Colorado mystique, immigrant history, tourism, family life, and general history, showing how beer lubricates (or does not) our lives.

Bock and Hanson argue that Colorado, the highest state, relishes "an enviable position at the pinnacle of brewing history." Reaching that summit has not always been a collaborative effort. Bock and Hanson tell a happier story today of the explosion in the number of beer outlets, which now even includes grocery stores. Breweries in various trade associations and at the Great American Beer Festival pursue fruitful collaborations. That harmonious picture is well told in these pages, which I join the authors to suggest swallowing with a pint in hand.

—THOMAS J. NOEL

ACKNOWLEDGEMENTS

Beer is best enjoyed in good company. We are grateful to all of the friends, tap hunters, brewers, and barflies who helped us write this book and create the exhibition that inspired it.

Thanks also to Allyson Brantley, B. Erin Cole, Elliott West, and Steve Danver for helping us make the case in the *Journal of the West* that beer is serious history, as well as to Tom Noel, Peter Kopp, Paul Sutter, Phoebe S.K. Young, Travis Rupp, Josh Berning, Mike McCullough, Kurt Gutjahr, and Patty Limerick for their fine taste in scholarship. We raise a glass to Ed Sealover and Jonathan Shikes and the many other journalists on the brew beat for their insightful coverage of Colorado's evolving beer business. We're grateful for our partners in brewing—Charlie Papazian, Gary Glass, Heidi Harris, and Karen Hertz—for sharing their time and their insider perspectives (and their beer!) and for making sure this book faithfully reflects the twists and turns of their careers in their chosen industry. To Mary Sullivan, Will Rempel, and Ryan Rebhan, thank you for your enthusiasm and encouragement and especially for doing a bunch of legwork to make sure that this book stands on a barrel of solid research.

We are deeply grateful for the members of the "Beer Here!" exhibition advisory committee. We feel so lucky to have such incredible colleagues—the History Colorado staff, volunteers, and interns who assisted with the research behind this project and the incredible team across the institution who brought "Beer Here!" to life in 2019. And special thanks to Steve Grinstead for making us sound smart, for wrangling our unruly footnotes, and for his good company and encouragement as this book took shape over the last decade. We owe you a beer, Steve.

A final and special thanks to our partners, Stacie Hanson and Laura Grims, for their indulgence and their willingness to spend vacations tracking down new breweries and tasting "this really interesting beer you might like." Cheers.

INTRODUCTION

Let's get this out of the way right at the outset: People brew good beer all over the country. So why a book about Colorado beer?

Well, for starters, Colorado is pouring a lot of beer these days. The state boasts more than 400 craft breweries (468 at the Brewers Association's most recent count), so it's possible to drink in a new spot every day of the year and not come close to getting around to all of them. Craft breweries account for most of the state's numbers, but Colorado is still the home of the Coors brewery—the biggest single-site brewery in North America. We host the Great American Beer Festival every fall. We're home to the Brewers Association and the American Homebrewers Association. So, by any measure, Colorado is one of the centers of (specific) gravity in the brewing world. But today's beer boom is only the most recent installment in a long saga of western suds.

Throughout Colorado's history, beer has mainly been an unpretentious and generally accessible beverage enjoyed by folks who aren't easily defined by geography, race, gender, or socioeconomic status. And that means it's a sort of magic potion for historians looking to make sense of the forces that have shaped everyday life in the Centennial State.

Beer's role in the gold rush shows us how saloons strengthened social bonds in Colorado's isolated mining communities. Beer was at the center of social reform during Prohibition, and it was the beverage Coloradans craved as the dry times drew to a close. By the middle of the twentieth century, beer had become emblematic of suburban shifts, and the way it was marketed in those "Mad Men" years shows how Coloradans thought about—and who was allowed access to—the American Dream. Beer was at the center of civil rights flashpoints, and to this day, some longtime Coloradans and newcomers alike align their choices at the bar with their political leanings. More recently, the craft beer boom was a dramatic sign of changing western economies. And the industry's ongoing recovery from the COVID-19 pandemic shows just how deeply embedded the local brewery has become in Colorado's culture.

So, again, why a book about Colorado beer? Well, it turns out that pint glasses make good lenses for surveying many of the key moments in our shared past because beer is more than a beverage in this state. It's something we seek in out-of-the-way places. It's a contentious topic we debate with our friends and family. It's an industry that employs thousands statewide. Beer helps us celebrate in the great outdoors and cozy up on cold winter nights, and it's a reason for communities to come together.

Our relationship with beer has changed over time, and that tells us something—lots of things, actually—about ourselves. It reveals how Coloradans used to live and what the ideal version of this place looked like to many of them. It tells us why a state founded in a saloon would enact Prohibition four years *before* the rest of the country and why, afterward, Colorado went on to become one of the best places in the world to enjoy a pint. From mining camps to today's booming cities, beer reveals an economy that relied on extraction evolving into one driven by tourism and recreation. It's a change putting Colorado at the forefront of an emerging New West—where people come for the outdoor lifestyle and stay for a few beers.

So come join us as we shine a light on Colorado's history, one pint at a time.

FIRST ROUND

LIQUID GOLD, 1859–1916[1]

This much we know with certainty: The story of the first beer brewed in Colorado did *not* happen anything like this.

As much as we may wish he had, a distinguished and industrious German brewmaster (let's call him Adolph) did not ride into town on an immaculate wagon pulled by a team of Clydesdale horses, doff his hat, and proclaim to the assembled townsfolk anything along these lines:

> *Ladies and gentlemen, I have long sought the perfect setting for brewing the world's best beer, and at last I have found it, right here. With limitless quantities of pure Rocky Mountain water, ideal agricultural conditions, and a reputation for discerning palates among its fine residents, I believe that this region is destined for an enviable position at the pinnacle of brewing history. I am fortunate to have arrived first, and henceforth and without ado I shall brew a beer worthy of the noble men and women who call this place home.*

Had they been able to peer a century and a half into the future, the first Euro-Americans to settle in the place we now call Colorado may well have concocted such an origin story for the local brewing industry—befitting a place that would one day boast such a robust beer scene. But lacking magical powers of foresight, the early settlers enjoyed those first pints without doing much to memorialize them. In fact, the real origin story of the Colorado brewing industry unfolded with little fanfare between the boom of the gold rush in 1859 and the early onset of Prohibition in 1916.

This means that historians and beer enthusiasts today (often one and the same) who want to illuminate the brewing industry's origins in Colorado must piece that story together

through sleuthing and archival legwork. What emerges from the past is not the heroic narrative that characterizes familiar pioneer stories. Rather, it's one of mining and agriculture, scientific advances and transportation revolutions—and, of course, booms and busts. It's a story of the American West that traces the bouncy, twisting, dusty trails of history that brought us to now.

BREWING AN INDUSTRY IN COLORADO

Ceran St. Vrain would have been an ideal founding figure for Colorado's brewers. A gentlemanly mountain man and one of the principal figures in the trading network centered on Bent's Fort in the 1830s and '40s, St. Vrain spent part of his boyhood in his family's St. Louis brewery before coming west.

In 1810, when Ceran St. Vrain was eight years old, his father opened one of the first breweries in St. Louis, selling strong ale to the thirsty cosmopolitan population of the United States' new city for "ten dollars a barrel in cash or twelve in produce" (around $200 cash or about $240 in produce in today's dollars; table beer could be had for half that price). Young Ceran was steeped in the business of brewing until the brewery burned down when he was eleven years old. With any hopes of inheriting the family business in ashes, St. Vrain shifted toward a new path that eventually led him to the Rocky Mountains in search of beaver pelts and the economic opportunities to be found on the western edge of American settlement.[2]

St. Vrain and the brothers Bent—the older Charles and younger William—built their eponymous fort in 1833 on the north bank of the Arkansas River, upstream from the mouth of the Purgatory, near present-day La Junta. The first American settlement in the land that would eventually come to be called Colorado, the trading post was an excellent place for commerce, sitting across the river from what was then part of Mexico. Indeed, Bent's Fort was a staging point for the U.S. Army's invasion of Mexico in 1846 at the outset of the Mexican-American War. From this headquarters, the members of Bent, St. Vrain, and Company made their fortunes purchasing bison robes from the region's buffalo hunters to bundle and send east, trading with local tribes including the Cheyenne and Arapaho, and catering to the needs of weary travelers on the Santa Fe Trail.

At Bent's Fort, people from many different cultures replenished necessities such as wagon parts, horseshoes, and firearms or indulged in luxuries hard to come by on the trail such as laundry and lemonade. But beer remained stubbornly unavailable. Bent's Fort featured no taproom within its adobe walls to offer travelers cool respite from sun and dust. In fact, the nearest beer cellar would have been hundreds of miles away.[3]

Ceran St. Vrain, whose family owned a brewery, would have made a fine founding figure for Colorado's beer industry. But he doesn't appear to have had any interest in the family business. *History Colorado Collection, 89.451.3435.*

Although mountain men and soldiers were known to sometimes brew personal stocks of beer using local flora, commercial brewing was not a viable business on the fur trade frontier.[4] Bulky and heavy to transport, with lower profit margins than distilled spirits and likely to spoil along the trail, beer was poorly suited for trade in the early nineteenth century since successful brewers needed a concentrated population of appreciative consumers nearby.

They also needed a reliable supply of grain and hops. St. Vrain saw the difficulties of securing reliable feedstock firsthand in St. Louis, as his father offered to trade beer for barley (twenty-four bushels for a barrel of strong beer) and other brewer's ingredients in order to ensure the next batch. An adequate supply of brewer's ingredients in places like Bent's Fort, where the global web of trade in Euro-American goods was spun down into a single long thread, was an even more daunting proposition.

Some Native people in the region, if not specifically in the place we now call Colorado, enjoyed fermented beverages resembling beer long before Euro-American settlers arrived. The Ancient Puebloans living in what we know today as southern Colorado and New Mexico appear to have brewed a beverage from fermented maize more than eight hundred years ago. Tribes throughout the Southwest, particularly in Arizona and Mexico, brewed "tiswin" or "tesguino" from corn and other available fermentable items; the drink is still a specialty of the Tarahumaras in northern Mexico. Euro-American explorers and traders occasionally tried to approximate the ales they longed for with local ingredients like pine needles and native grains and roots, using crude homebrewing processes. But the industry that would become today's booming brewery scene arrived in Colorado with the earliest Argonauts of the gold rush.[5]

Throughout the first half of the nineteenth century, beer remained a local product and a city product, typically available only where the economy and population were robust enough to ensure a steady supply chain and an adequate customer base. So beer was rarely available west of St. Louis before gold strikes in California and Colorado set off a series of mineral rushes that dotted the region with new settlements. These mineral rushes conjured urban centers like Denver into being with previously unimaginable speed, and with cities suddenly in place, brewers were quick to take advantage of a growing market.

The story of the beer industry in Colorado—the *real* story, unobscured by mythology and nostalgia—begins in Las Vegas, New Mexico, where a man named Frederick Z. Solomon operated a mercantile store with his brother. Near the beginning of 1859, Solomon was in St. Louis buying new stock for his trading post when he heard news of a gold strike along the South Platte River and its tributaries. The twenty-nine-year-old Polish Jewish immigrant quickly decided that his future was among the hopeful miners flocking to the Rockies, so he teamed up with Joseph Doyle, a trader who had been operating in the Arkansas River Valley and south into New Mexico for nearly two decades. Solomon returned west with a large wagon train of supplies, and in the summer of 1859, he set up shop in the town of Auraria on today's Larimer Street. His general store sat just across Cherry Creek from the still-separate settlement of Denver City, under the banner of J.B. Doyle & Company.[6]

John Good watched Solomon set up his business from his own mercantile shop on Blake Street near Fifteenth Street on the Denver City side of Cherry Creek. The twenty-four-year-old immigrant from the German-speaking region of Alsace-Lorraine had arrived in May, one month before Solomon, riding an ox cart loaded with supplies to sell to the hopeful miners on their way to the booming gold diggings. Setting out from Akron, Ohio, he had crossed the plains alone; without a partner like Doyle to help capitalize his enterprise, Good was obliged to make regular resupply trips back east by himself. It was a trip that sometimes took him three months.[7]

When Solomon and Good looked out over the town that would become Denver during that summer of 1859, they saw a dusty, rambunctious settlement convulsively developing into the main supply depot for the mining camps scattered throughout the mountains to the west. A growing community of businessmen and women in Denver and Auraria offered food, preserves, equipment, clothing, lodging, assorted entertainments, and plenty of the pungent Taos Lightning whiskey that was often available for purchase with pinches of gold dust measured out on the scales saloons kept sitting on the bar.[8] But as had been the case at Bent's Fort, one item not yet available at any price was beer.

We know that both Solomon and Good quickly recognized a market for brew along the Rocky Mountain mining frontier. But we don't know precisely how they got the ingredients. The historical record here is a little threadbare, and so historians must play detective. We know that before the year's end, Solomon and a business partner named Charles Tascher founded the Rocky Mountain Brewery, and by the spring of 1860, Good's name was associated with the enterprise as well. But beer is a product of the special alchemy between barley, hops, yeast, and water. How did Solomon and his partners assemble these ingredients in a dusty boomtown in 1859?

One story, apparently based on tradition more than any firm documentation, claims that John Good brought the first hops to Denver in

Frederick Z. Salomon and Charles Tascher opened the Rocky Mountain Brewery in Auraria at Tenth and St. Louis (Larimer) Streets, selling their first beers in December 1859 to good reviews from thirsty newspaper editors and miners. Shown here is the brewery's second location, which opened with a lagering cellar in 1861 in today's Highland neighborhood. No one bothered to record much about the first site. *History Colorado Collection, 83.130.14.*

his ox cart.[9] If so, it seems likely that he carried them on his second trip, made around the beginning of autumn 1859 to resupply his store and prepare for winter.[10] Good then sold the hops to Solomon, perhaps as previously arranged. Alternatively, Solomon might have bought the hops on a quick, unrecorded purchasing trip to St Louis.[11] Or they may have arrived with a speculative freighter. The transport of the yeast is even less documented—which is to say that it is not recorded anywhere—but the hop merchant could have carried both yeast and hops to Colorado. It's even possible that the brewers cultivated their yeast from a local source.

Whether these key ingredients were sourced via an undocumented purchasing trip or from an enterprising merchant, what *is* clear is that once Fred Solomon got his hands on hops and yeast, he'd cleared the major hurdles. With water supplied from the South Platte River, he started brewing in what could charitably be identified as a shed near his store on the east side of today's Larimer Street—between Tenth and Eleventh—right in the center of what is now the Auraria Higher Education Campus in downtown Denver.[12]

Finding a ready market for his brew in the ever-growing outpost that was Denver, Solomon soon brought Tascher on as his partner in the Rocky Mountain Brewery. Charles Tascher arrived in December 1858 as a hopeful prospector in Colorado, which was then being called the Jefferson Territory by the miners and Euro-American settlers who showed little interest in what tribal nations such as the Arapaho, Cheyenne, and Ute called their homelands. He was one of the lucky few who made good in the goldfields, discovering the Bates mine, a major lode in the Gregory Diggings near present-day Central City. Solomon may have brought Tascher into the brewery enterprise as an investor, but it appears that he was an active partner at the outset, delivering kegs around town and perhaps even doing the brewing.[13]

By late November, William Byers, the grateful editor of the *Rocky Mountain News*, was able to thank the publicity-savvy brewers in print for the gift of a "huge bottle of this teutonic beverage, the first ever brewed in the Territory of Jefferson," which would soon be available to the public. Two weeks later, Tascher delivered a whole keg to the *News* office, and the editors promptly pronounced it, somewhat curiously, "a little the best we ever tasted." A week after that, a notice ran that the beer would be for sale that weekend. Orders were duly placed at J.B. Doyle & Company, Solomon's employer, which was apparently happy to support the enterprise and add another line of business.[14]

Recalling that joyful occasion years later, one eloquent early imbiber recounted that the original Colorado beer, "though quite drinkable, was as innocent of hops as our early whiskey was of wheat or rye."[15] "Quite drinkable" was good enough for the thirsty residents of the new territory, and the Rocky Mountain Brewery prospered. Only one month after opening, Solomon announced plans to build a beer cellar across the South Platte to expand capacity.

Despite the brewery's quick success, it was not enough to keep Tascher tethered, and he left the business the following spring. Solomon then brought on John Good and Charles Endlich in a new partnership that lasted until Solomon himself moved on to other ventures in 1861, rising to prominence as a key figure in many of Denver's early water companies and railroad enterprises. After Endlich died in 1864, Good continued to operate the brewery until 1871 before selling it to his brewmaster, Philip Zang, and redirecting his attention and capital to banking and real estate investment.[16]

Colorado's first brewers were not the romantic figures that often grace the creation myths of frontier enterprises. When Philip Zang took over the Rocky Mountain Brewery and eponymously rechristened it the Philip Zang Brewery, he was the first trained professional beermaker to pour water over barley in the Centennial State. Rather than impassioned artisans who carried their craft westward in covered wagons to worthy pioneers, the men who set Colorado on a course to becoming one of the hubs of the global craft brewing industry were savvy businessmen—not so different from Ceran St. Vrain in that respect—who saw beer as one opportunity among a diverse portfolio of ventures that they could undertake to attain their fortunes in the wide-open gold rush–era economy.

The tale of Colorado's first brewery may not be the sort of dramatic or colorful origin story that makes for a good yarn along the bar. And in that respect—the ordinariness of its arrival amid countless other enterprises during the tumult of the gold rush—it went largely unremarked and unrecorded even by those who were there. In this way, the coming of the beer industry as we recognize it today is importantly different from so many other events in western history that were mythologized in real time. And that can make beer a valuable lens on economy and lifestyle during the gold rush and beyond.

In other words, if you look deeply into a pint of your favorite Colorado beer, you might catch a glimpse of the state's golden past, unobscured by all the glitter.

THE ALL-PURPOSE SALOON

Like most of the hopeful men (and they were almost all men) who arrived in Colorado with the gold rush, Colorado's first brewers probably didn't envision a long-term stay in the West. The vast majority of gold-seekers arriving in Denver in the summer of 1858 were, by the summer of 1859, "go backers," returning empty-handed to Midwestern American cities and despondent that the rumors of gold hadn't panned out in the way they'd hoped. But unlike the fate of these disappointed and often destitute would-be miners striking out in the Colorado Gold Rush, the *liquid* gold rush was starting to put cash in pockets. And as breweries on the Rocky Mountain mining frontier popped up, so too did the saloons where the majority of beers were consumed.

Saloons moved west just as quickly as the miners did, and they were the first stop for thousands of thirsty gold-seekers after a long trek over the dusty plains. At a time when gold drove the economy and saloons were the only buildings in town, saloon owners across the state accepted glittering flakes of gold dust in exchange for glasses of whiskey or beer, and plenty of new arrivals spent their first nights in Colorado sleeping on saloon floors. For many who staked their claims and sought their fortunes on the mining frontier, saloons were a welcome retreat even when they were little more than canvas tents stretched over some rough-hewn logs. The term *saloon* entered the American lexicon in the 1840s as a more respectable substitute for the public house or tavern, which had acquired vice-ridden reputations. But as the term moved to the remote mining camps of the Mountain West,

Canvas tents and barrels passed for bars in Colorado's early saloons. If a gold strike proved out, saloons were often the first permanent buildings in town. *History Colorado Collection, 2000.129.178.*

its association with sophisticated French salons grew harder and harder to discern. Western saloons were typically pragmatic (read: slapdash) affairs designed with the singular objective of commencing service as quickly as possible. Some early proprietors went to the trouble of setting up a tent for the comfort of their customers, but the clientele—mostly miners—weren't especially picky: an open-air saloon could work just as well.

Town building was one of the first orders of business when a gold strike proved out, and saloons were usually the first buildings to go up. In the absence of any other civic infrastructure, local watering holes were hubs of social and economic activity—vital to nearly every aspect of life in a remote and yet-to-be-developed part of the growing nation.

The first saloon along Cherry Creek in what would become Denver arrived with a well-known merchant named Richens Lacy Wootton, who rolled into town on Christmas Eve 1858. Wootton was ready to get right to business, simply setting a row of barrels on end to serve as a bar and tapping a keg of potent Taos Lightning whiskey in the back of one of his wagons. The sudden saloonkeeper proceeded to hand out free holiday drinks, and soon the appreciative residents were calling him "Uncle Dick" and offering him free town lots along Ferry Street in Auraria to set up a proper saloon.[17]

When "Uncle Dick" Wootton opened his Western Hall early in 1859, just a few months after that first holiday toast, the building greeting eager customers was constructed of hewn logs stacked one and a half stories high and covered with a shake shingle roof. The roof was a real marker of distinction. Other proprietors, such as Wootton's competitors at the Denver House, still hedged their investment by eschewing the complication of roof building and (not unlike future airport architects) instead stretched canvas over a peaked frame.[18] Proprietors in more remote camps followed the Denver House model, relying on stretched canvas to keep out the elements well into the 1870s. Even gold-seekers arriving in Leadville in 1879 found a camp city where few (if any) residents built structures with a view toward doing business beyond the end of the month.[19] Haphazard and unplanned, mountain towns and their saloons reflected the transience of the residents and the boom-and-bust cycles of the gold rush.

If a gold strike in some remote mountain valley did prove out, however, saloonkeepers might upgrade their tents to a wooden structure. Notched logs or boards and nails evidenced a barman's confidence in a town's economic future, and glass windows or wooden floors brought some of the comforts of city life to the mining frontier. In these early stages of growth, even

Just a few miles above the town of Creede lay the Holy Moses saloon. Named for the nearby mine, it was among the first watering holes in town. Pictured here in the 1890s, saloon owner William Orthen (*right, in shirtsleeves*) had invested in the trappings of permanence—glass windows, wooden walkway, even a roof—that indicated his mountain mining town was there to stay. *Courtesy of Denver Public Library Special Collections, X-7488.*

rudimentary saloons were among the most prominent buildings in town, and residents looked to them to fill multiple roles. Many saloons doubled as hotels for newcomers with nowhere else to go, and accommodations ranged from a cot upstairs to a pile of straw on the floor once the revelry died down. Miners arriving at the saloon in Gregory's Diggings (modern-day Central City) in 1861 found three tents joined together with a handmade bar and gambling tables taking up most of the indoor space, leaving enough room for a tray of baked goods and even a barber's chair.[20]

The multi-role saloon was common in gold rush towns, and depending on a community's needs, saloons also served as courthouses, theaters, newspaper offices, general stores, and as churches on Sunday mornings. On occasion, they were even legislative chambers: Denver's first city government met at the Apollo Hall saloon near today's Fourteenth and Larimer Streets, and territorial lawmakers followed suit, moving their deliberations between saloons in Denver and Golden when the Colorado Territory was established in 1861. Indeed, by 1870, Denver boasted six churches, four schools, two hospitals, one library, and three banks. But as historian Thomas J. Noel notes, the total number of all civic institutions combined still equaled only one-third of the forty-eight saloons frequented by the city's 4,759 residents—a striking ratio of more than one saloon for every 100 people. It wasn't until Prohibition that non-drinking establishments outnumbered saloons in the city.[21]

If fortune smiled on Colorado's miners and they struck it rich, business owners in thriving cities upgraded their establishments to reflect growing prosperity and the roots those miners were setting down in the West. Successful operators replaced wood and canvas with brick and stone (sometimes incentivized by catastrophic fires, as when Denver burned in 1863), and the amenities of urban life took on more refinement. Proper hotels and churches sprang up, and the owners of existing saloons made improvements to keep pace with the rest of the city—applying plaster over rough interior walls and installing dedicated beer taps on ornate bars with brass rails in place of planks or barrels. Some owners even added second stories or constructed urban-looking façades to lure residents inside. Beer professionally brewed in Colorado and beyond flowed liberally in saloons by the middle of the 1870s, and it rapidly replaced the rotgut whiskey and watery grog that miners made do with in the early years of the mining rush. Soon beer drinking became a custom even for upscale saloon clientele, and the unquenchable thirst for fresh beer only deepened.

By the latter decades of the nineteenth century, upgraded old stalwarts were competing with a new class of saloon purpose-built from the start to embody the opulence of western wealth. These elegant new establishments—often celebrated in the local papers as objects of civic pride—occupied prominent locations and large lots. They catered to more upscale clientele, with enormous gilt mirrors reflecting patrons leaning on polished bars or testing their luck on mechanical slots or ornate gaming tables as they enjoyed refined beverages. Games of chance lined the walls of almost every saloon, and the most upscale may have offered well-

A so-called tied house served only one brewery's beer, acting as a dedicated outlet and advertisement while offering assurances of supply for the saloon owner. But sometimes these arrangements saddled the proprietor with crippling debts and a struggling business. *Courtesy of Denver Public Library Special Collections, X-10481.*

appointed private rooms for their elite patrons to relax and gamble in, tucked away from the hoi polloi.[22]

While saloons made efforts to distinguish themselves in terms of the quality of their furnishings and offerings, patrons often divided themselves according to race or ethnic origin. In more populous communities, German, Irish, Scandinavian, Italian, Eastern European, Latino, and African American patrons could relax amid the fellowship of other men with similar backgrounds and cultural customs away from the prejudiced society outside. At the right saloons, men far from home could comfortably converse in their native language, receive mail, share news from home, get leads on work opportunities, and enjoy the camaraderie and diversions that were hard for them to come by elsewhere in American society.[23]

More than one sociologist at the time ascribed the saloon's popularity to its role as the "workingman's club," and one astutely observed that the saloon owed its success to adeptly meeting customers' needs:

> *It is an institution grown up among the people, not only in answer to their demand for wares, but to their demand for certain necessities and conveniences, which it supplies, either alone or better than any other agency.*

Two out of every three saloonkeepers were immigrants, and many saloons served as ethnic community centers. In a place like the Scandinavian House saloon in Denver, patrons could speak their native languages and enjoy a brief reminder of home. *Courtesy of the Denver Public Library Special Collections,* X-22489.

> *It is part of the neighborhood, which must change with the neighborhood; it fulfills in it the social functions which unfortunately have been left to it to exercise. With keen insight into human nature and into the wants of the people, it anticipates all other agencies in supplying them, and thus claims its right to existence.*[24]

Indeed, saloons regularly went well beyond simply supplying a few pleasant hours of respite for their patrons. Many filled critical economic, political, and social roles in their communities. Some saloonkeepers cashed paychecks, offered loans, and stored valuables in the safe for patrons with limited access to or understanding of the banking system. Others shepherded the formation of fraternal organizations to guarantee that countrymen and their families were insured against the hazards of their dangerous occupations and received proper burials when tragedy struck. Likewise, saloons provided laborers with space for union meetings and even served as de facto headquarters during strikes. John Popovich's Slovenian Gardens saloon in Denver's Globeville neighborhood became a rallying point during the 1903 smelter workers' strike until police raided it and closed the community's other saloons.

With their saloons occupying such a central place in the lives of their communities, saloonkeepers were, unsurprisingly, also often active in politics, organizing voters and delivering victory for sometimes unscrupulous politicians whose money greased saloon owners' palms. Seeing opportunity in their local popularity and a chance to secure favorable laws, many owners served on city councils and other legislative entities themselves.[25]

Operating a saloon was a reasonably surefire way to make a buck compared to the uncertain and dangerous mining business, and it was a pathway to economic security for many hopeful migrants chasing the American Dream out west. In fact, most saloon owners on the Rocky Mountain mining frontier came west searching for gold but made their way behind the bar to escape the tedium and poverty that came with a life panning for shiny dust in freezing mountain streams. "Mining the miners" at the bar was a much more reliable way to make a living. Even those owners who struggled to make ends meet found brewers ready to keep their dreams alive by assuming their debts—and maybe even funding new décor and other improvements—in exchange for exclusively selling that brewer's beer. These so-called tied

Ornate décor including wallpaper and a cigar humidor (not to mention beer on tap) at the White House Saloon in the Cripple Creek Mining District brought an air of sophistication to the mining frontier. *Courtesy of Denver Public Library Special Collections, X-661.*

houses trapped some operators in debt that they were never able to pay off, but for many saloon owners—among whom 40 percent had emigrated from foreign countries—pouring beer or working as a mixologist (a term that dates to the late nineteenth century) was a pathway to the middle class.

In a society focused on pulling gold out of the ground and not much else, diversions were extremely important, and successful saloonkeepers had to be pillars of the community—popular not just for their ability to keep the drinks flowing but also for the warm and welcoming atmosphere they fostered from behind the bar. With every saloon offering the same wares and sporting the same games of chance, watering holes had to find ways to differentiate themselves to survive. One of the most effective ways of doing so was by employing a barman who could cultivate the personal relationships that maintained a steady clientele. Thus saloonkeepers had to be affable and jolly while also capable of holding their own in a ragged-edged world. They were, generally speaking, men who you'd want to have a beer with—good storytellers or good liars (often one and the same) with whom you could spend a few pleasant hours or drown your sorrows.[26]

Décor in all classes of saloon reflected the patriarchal atmosphere of frontier society and the imperial project of American expansion. Saloon walls almost invariably featured portraits of virile prizefighters, stately presidents, classically styled feminine figures, brewers' advertisements with tantalizing Victorian women, taxidermied hunting trophies, and patriotic scenes from American history. The most common sight in any American saloon between 1896 and the onset of Prohibition was F. Otto Becker's lithograph *Custer's Last Fight* (based on Cassilly Adams's original painting), portraying the Battle of the Greasy Grass, or, as it is also known, the Battle of the Little Bighorn. The Anheuser-Busch Brewing Company distributed this artistic celebration of one of the most violent episodes in the conquest of the American West, seeking to appeal to the testosterone-soaked barroom clientele by linking Budweiser to perceptions of heroism and glory that many Americans associated with the event at the time. Budweiser distributed more than 150,000 reproductions as patriotic advertising, making it arguably one of the most well-known pieces of art in the United States save for Gilbert Stuart's portrait of George Washington on the dollar bill.

Taken together, interior decorating in saloons amounted to a style that historian Elliott West has dubbed "Victorian macho." These nineteenth-century man caves were a world in which women were not welcome.[27] While women might occasionally attend theater and other entertainment events at saloons, the usual patrons were almost exclusively men since societal norms

Custer's Last Fight, the famous (or infamous) depiction of the Battle of the Greasy Grass/Battle of the Little Bighorn, is one of the most viewed pieces of American art save for Gilbert Stuart's portrait of George Washington on the dollar bill. *History Colorado Collection, H.5904.2.*

of the day, generally speaking, frowned on respectable women drinking in public. As Frederick Neef, a saloonkeeper and brewer in Denver, recalled, "Now and then a woman would come to the rear door and buy a pint of whisky, but they never lounged in the saloon. No respectable woman would drink in public."[28]

A woman wary of her social reputation who wanted a beer had few options to slake her thirst in Colorado. Depending on where she lived, bottled beer may not have been readily available, meaning that women who wanted to savor a beer at home were sometimes beholden to the saloon. Some might "rush the growler," bringing (or sending a child with) a pail or bottle to be filled discreetly at the saloon and consumed later. Some might also visit a beer garden, as German brewers in the latter decades of the nineteenth century imported the custom of drinking beer in family-friendly and pleasant outdoor settings. Some of these gardens, like Adolph Coors's Golden Grove, provided shady respites near their breweries where

SALTED
BUTTER CORN

Opposite, top: Saloons like this one in Leadville were commonly filled with games of chance and decorated in a style historian Elliott West has described as "Victorian macho." *Courtesy of Denver Public Library Special Collections, X-294.*

Opposite, bottom: Interior view of the Tollgate Saloon in Blackhawk, Colorado, in the 1890s. The décor (and stains on the floor) would have been typical of the state's more ornate saloons as mining outposts like Blackhawk transformed into cities and towns later in the nineteenth century. *Courtesy of Denver Public Library Special Collections, X-2012.*

Above: Families enjoying a picnic with Neef Gold Belt Beer in a Denver park in the early 1900s. Outdoor beer drinking was understood as a different, more socially acceptable activity for respectable women and families than the kind of imbibing done in saloons. *History Colorado Collection, 90.152.40.*

entire families could enjoy their beer together in a respectable, open atmosphere. But by and large, most beer was enjoyed in saloons in settings that excluded women.[29]

This glaring exclusion would come back to haunt saloon operators and brewers, but for the first half century of American settlement in Colorado, business was good. From Denver to Leadville, Central City to Creede, and everywhere in between, saloons provided a foundation on which town social life was built, particularly among the predominantly male population of prospectors who rushed to each new mineral strike. And with more and more men arriving in Colorado, saloons had little trouble selling all the beer the state's brewers could brew.

But growing a business on the edge of an expanding nation came with its own set of challenges, and Colorado's fledgling beer industry was still subject to the whims of international trade and the West's arid climate. Change was on the horizon for these brewers who, like their nascent home state, were increasingly connected to a network of international commerce—a network that shaped everything from the price of beer to the way it was made, well into the next century.

LAGER RISES TO THE TOP

By the middle of the 1870s, Colorado's population was booming, and with the number of thirsty Coloradans growing by the day, brewers raced to stay a step ahead of the demand. Colorado brewers statewide produced nearly 23,000 barrels of beer (at thirty-one gallons per barrel) in 1878, and for a decade and a half, the state's output just kept growing. By early 1893, Colorado's twenty-three breweries were producing nearly 235,000 barrels—more than a tenfold increase in fifteen years—before that year's major economic recession forced the industry to slow down. Coors Brewing Company had enjoyed expansions of capacity and infrastructure from its founding in 1873 through the depression of 1893. Other large-scale brewers, like Walter Brewing Company in Pueblo, set up shop and set about making beer on an industrial scale—just one of many major enterprises helping propel Colorado's explosive economic growth.[30]

This twenty-year expansion reflected changing preferences among thirsty American consumers, the growing reach of supply chains as Colorado integrated more fully into the national and global economy, and the growth of American manufacturing in general during the Industrial Revolution. But the biggest factor driving the industry's growth was the new lager-style beer introduced by German immigrants in the years following the Civil War. Lighter in flavor and lower in alcohol, lager captured palates across the nation, sweeping aside the distilled spirits and cider that had been the cornerstone of American drinking habits since colonial times.

Lager differs from ale in ways that still make it the beer of choice for thirsty Americans. Both styles of beer use barley, hops, water, and yeast as their primary ingredients. But that's where the similarities usually end. In contrast to the warmth-loving microbes brewers use to make ale, lager yeast thrives in the cold. Ale yeast tends to be buoyant—forming a sludgy crown on the top of the fermenting beer—while lager yeast likes to do its job from below. Ale is typically fermented for two to four weeks and then served immediately or packaged for distribution and consumption. Lager, by contrast, needs to be rested, or "lagered," for a period of several weeks or months, during which time proteins fall to the bottom of the barrel to leave behind a clearer beer with more delicate flavors that, for many, tends to be less filling than ale.

For most of Colorado's early beer drinkers, top-fermenting English-style ales like porter, stout, and bitters were all they knew—the English drinking tradition, and the beer that went along with it, had informed Americans' notions of what beer was since the settlement of the first colonies. But the varying quality of some ales and their tendency to quickly spoil pushed tipplers in the early republic into a preference for whiskey and rum over beer, even when beer was available. That changed in the middle of the nineteenth century as more and more lager-loving German immigrants made their way to the United States. They arrived in a world thirsty for something new.[31]

The end of the Civil War in 1865 and the arrival of the railroad in Denver five years later brought a new, steady stream of arrivals to Colorado as immigrants from all over the world swelled the ranks of those bellying up to bars along the Front Range. Beginning in 1870, railcars started disgorging a new generation of immigrants, and the city's population boomed. The number of people calling Denver home shot up from 4,759 in 1870 to 35,692 in 1880 on its way to 106,713 in 1890 and 213,318 in 1910.[32]

As in other western mining rushes, these new residents conjured forth a metropolis so quickly that historians sometimes call their settlements "instant cities." Many mining camps and their supply hubs followed this pattern, skipping straight past the more bucolic phases of development to give the towns an urban character right from the start. City builders quickly saw the need for organizing local governments that could provide law enforcement, fire protection, sanitation, and the other services that smoothed the rough edges of urban living—roles previously filled by saloons. Civic leaders recognized the need to provide amenities like schools, theaters, and churches in order to attract the families and businesses that could ensure permanence for their city should the gold and silver give out. And entrepreneurs like

Early Colorado mining towns were ethnically diverse. While many saloons served as enclaves for immigrants from specific countries, others like this one in Georgetown, Colorado, served as meeting places for laborers from across the globe. *Courtesy of the Denver Public Library Special Collections, X-6549.*

newspaper editors, clothiers, and grocers—not to mention brewers and saloon operators—located their businesses among these clusters of potential customers, providing the added refinements of city life. Foreign-born immigrants were often attracted to the increased opportunity of city economies, making for a remarkably diverse population in many western outposts from the very beginning.[33]

As the most connected supply hub and urban center for hundreds of miles, Denver and the mining camps it supplied had a thirst for beer that outpaced even the high-country mining towns with their own extraordinary population growth. The *Rocky Mountain News Weekly* claimed that beer consumption in Denver more than doubled in the first few years of the 1870s alone. A beer cost anywhere from a nickel to fifteen cents depending on the establishment, and some Denver saloons drained ten kegs a day in the hot summer months.[34]

Through the first half of the nineteenth century, the U.S. brewing industry had remained relatively small, struggling even in St. Louis up to the 1840s, when that Midwestern city's three breweries produced only about

3,000 barrels annually. Around 1842, a German immigrant named William Lemp introduced lager beer to the city, and it quickly became the favorite drink in saloons, particularly in the summer. By 1854, St. Louis, by then the eighth-largest city in the nation, boasted twenty-four breweries that turned out a combined 60,000 barrels of beer that year, and still the lager ran out by September. By 1860, forty breweries were producing 189,000 barrels of beer annually in St. Louis, a number the Colorado brewers wouldn't catch up with for nearly thirty years.

Not that Colorado brewers didn't do everything they could to catch up more quickly, and the mining camps that fanned out across the mountains after the Russell Party's 1858 gold strike along the South Platte River were well supplied with liquid gold. By 1860, the *Rocky Mountain News* correspondent from the Gregory mining district was boasting, "Lager beer is behind many of our bars." When he toured Colorado in 1866, travel writer Bayard Taylor noted the popularity of the brew, observing that saloons boasting "lager beer" signs were prominent along the cacophonous road up Gregory Gulch from Black Hawk to Central City.[35]

It took a lot of beer—and thus a lot of barley and hops—to supply all those saloons and slake the prodigious thirst of residents in burgeoning communities in the mountains. Colorado's early brewers did everything they could to procure ingredients for their beer, but then as now, the demand from Colorado beer drinkers far outpaced the state's agricultural capacity. The Colorado brewing industry's first liquid gold rush was propelled not by the region's natural suitability to beer production but by the extension of supply chains that could reliably bring manufacturers the ingredients they needed.

Even with a market thirsty for all they could make, Colorado's early brewers struggled to make ends meet amid the challenges of operating a business on the edge of the national economy. In 1865, rising commodity prices forced several breweries—including the Rocky Mountain Brewery, Sigi's Colorado Brewery, and the Ale Brewery—to collusively raise the price of eight-gallon kegs by one dollar (an increase of nearly 15 percent) due to "the extreme high price of ale brewers' stock." In a region where short growing seasons, weather extremes, and arduous travel routes could make basic necessities scarce and expensive, procuring enough of the "ale brewers' stock" to satisfy customers was a consistent and costly challenge in Colorado during the state's first decades.[36]

Several breweries developed seed programs aimed at cultivating an ample (and contracted) local supply. As early as 1874, the Denver Brewing

Beers and bikes have long gone hand in hand here in Colorado. These dapper gents posed for this photo in a Denver park just before the onset of state prohibition in 1916. *History Colorado Collection, 90.52.305.*

Company offered seed barley to farmers at cost with a promise to buy all they could grow. In 1892, Adolph Zang (son of founder Philip Zang) boasted that the brewery had been "largely instrumental in starting the cultivation of barley by Colorado farmers, frequently furnishing the seed to the farmer on a year's time, and in some cases giving him instructions as to the best methods of cultivation." As the biggest brewery in the region, with a barley bill of about $100,000 (more than $3.3 million in today's dollars) to produce around 150,000 barrels annually, Zang had good reason to promote advantageous local agricultural arrangements.[37]

Brewers like Adolph Coors in Golden and Samuel Pells in Boulder continued such efforts up to the eve of Prohibition.[38] In fact, as Pells looked ahead to the spring of 1907, the president of the Crystal Springs Brewing and Ice Company had two big problems: Prohibition was on the local ballot, and barley was in short supply. The trick was discerning which was the greater threat. Temperance advocates were supporting a "Better Boulder" slate of city council candidates who promised to dry up saloons within the city limits. But Pells judged the more pressing concern to be securing the barley he needed to continue brewing his popular lineup of weurzbergers, extra pales, and Bohemian lagers.

As the election drew near, Pells advertised his intention to take a break from the campaign and travel east to purchase several carloads of barley seed, which he would "distribute among the farmers of this section" in time for spring planting "in the hopes that a better character of barley will result." Explaining that a "peculiarly pure quality of it is required for malt and the brewers want the best," Pells promised to furnish the seed at his cost and pay a "good price" to growers who would contract their crop to Crystal Springs.[39]

Although Colorado's early brewers often had to go to great lengths—sometimes literally—to secure ingredients, brewers and boosters alike sang the praises of the "superior quality" of Colorado's barley.[40] Still, limited local supplies and high prices consistently forced those brewers to look farther afield to secure all the grain they needed. An 1873 article in the *Rocky Mountain News* put it bluntly: "There is not enough barley raised in Colorado to supply the beer brewers with malt."[41]

Despite the apparent opportunity this shortfall might have created for local barley growers, at the end of the 1874 growing season a farmer named W.D. Arnett of Bear Creek near Morrison, wrote to the *Colorado Transcript* that he had "quit the cultivation of barley because the market was so limited that I had hard work to sell." The *Rocky Mountain News* in Denver reprinted the letter with skeptical commentary, but Arnett's experience suggests a mismatch in the local market.[42] Large maltsters in the Midwest—with increasingly efficient railroad links to Colorado—could compete economically with small local growers who often had to cart their bushels (sometimes over mountain passes) to brewers, who then had to do their own processing and malting.

Malting, the process of steeping and germinating grain to get at the sugars within, was a time-consuming, labor- and space-intensive process. Some brewers—notably Adolph Coors, whose grand aspirations and belief in quality assurance through vertical integration led him to build a malthouse next to the brewhouse, preferred to malt their own barley. But most looked to reduce costs where they could, and as a writer for the *Rocky Mountain News* explained in 1873, "When barley rises to $1.25 per bushel here, it is cheaper for our brewers to purchase ready-made malt at the east and ship it to Denver. This can be readily, and constantly, done."[43]

And so, busy brewers trying to maximize production increasingly turned to these national operators to smooth out kinks in their supply chains.

Difficult as it was for brewers to get an adequate supply of barley from local sources, hops posed a steeper challenge. The first Rocky Mountain Brewery lager had been "innocent of hops" because the bitter and aromatic cone-shaped flowers were difficult and expensive to obtain. In what may be a rare example of mythologizing about those first beers, legend has it that John Good earned his partnership in the Rocky Mountain Brewery by hauling the first hops across the plains in his ox cart unaccompanied.[44] Under such circumstances, prudent brewers used just as much as they had to in order to stretch the supply as far as they could.

Much as they had with barley, beer-loving newspaper editors and brewers prodded the state's farmers to plant hops. In 1892, Adolph Zang lamented in the local press, "As it has been demonstrated that hops can be successfully and very profitable [*sic*] grown in Colorado, it seems a pity that more hops are not locally grown so as to more fully meet the local demand."[45] The newspapers of the day do contain a few mentions of enterprising farmers planting hop fields along the Front Range. In 1875, a man named C.J. Marsh planted twenty acres of hops on Bear Creek near Morrison.[46] And in 1889, the *Silver Cliff Rustler* reported, "There is a twenty-two-acre field of hops near Denver which will produce this year 1,500 pounds to the acre."[47] But Zang's claims are dubious.

Hops never took hold as a commodity crop in Colorado, much to the frustration of the editor of the *Fort Collins Weekly Courier*, who in 1911 exhorted in a headline "Hop Growing Is Profitable: Farmers in State of Washington Making Big Money from Their Hop Fields—Why Not Start Industry Here?" The writer went on to offer an overview of the lucrative hop harvest in the Yakima Valley in Washington State, which he calculated was worth roughly $1.2 million. However, he failed to mention that the longer summer days and ideal climatic conditions of the Pacific Northwest made for much higher yields than could be obtained in Colorado.[48]

Hops are still hard to grow—and thus obtain—locally in Colorado, and like Colorado brewers today, their forerunners turned to suppliers in New

This watercolor depicts the Coors brewery as it looked in 1884, about a decade after Adolph Coors and Jacob Schueler repurposed an old tannery along the banks of Clear Creek in Golden, Colorado. *Courtesy of the Coors Archive.*

York, the Pacific Northwest, and particularly Europe to meet their needs.[49] While homegrown barley and hops were praised, some brewers advertised their exotic foreign hops as a sign of quality since the public associated imported goods with better quality and sophistication. Zang's boasted in its advertisements that the beer was "[b]rewed exclusively of Bohemian Hops

and Selected Colorado Barley," and the Palace Bar in Creede crowed that it was the "Sole Handlers of the Coors Beer. The finest Beer in the State. Made from Imported hops."[50]

As with barley, the difficulty of growing hops wasn't only climatic but also logistical and economic. "The finest quality of hops in the country are grown in Colorado," an "eminent Milwaukee brewer" told a Colorado newspaperman in 1889 (in an article that smacks of reality-stretching boosterism). "But the freight rates are so unreasonable that we cannot afford to buy them here. We can get the German hops a trifle cheaper. The Colorado hops are equally good, but then the competition in beer making is so great that we have to buy where we can save a penny. Cheap ocean transportation more than overcomes the duty laid on hops."[51] Whether or not the eminent Milwaukee brewer was real or just a contrived mouthpiece for the author of the article, the challenges of competing in a national and global hop marketplace deterred efforts to grow hops along Colorado's Front Range. Despite the local thirst for beer, hops were never a significant crop in Colorado fields before Prohibition.

The decades-long expansion of Colorado's brewing industry that started in the 1870s show us how Colorado's economy was knitted into the fabric of international economies. As Coloradans' palates increasingly craved refreshing lagers popularized by German immigrants, the industry transitioned from relying on local growers to national and international supply chains. And as the Industrial Revolution took hold, brewers kept availing themselves of new technologies and opportunities that allowed them to brew more beer and ship it farther from home.

Industry came to Colorado by design, as an intended outcome of westward expansion and the rise of global capitalism. Although Colorado beer and brewing were just small pieces of this global story, they were some of the most telling changes in the daily lives of recently arrived Coloradans thirsty to bring the trappings of home to the Rockies.

BREWERS GO BIG

A cottage industry for most of its time on Earth, brewing has primarily been the purview of women and done in the home. But professionalization, capitalization, and mechanization of the brewing industry over the course of the nineteenth century reconfigured the ways American beer was made and which Americans were making it.

The historical record is clear that women have, until comparatively recently, always been key figures in the art of fermentation. An ode to the Sumerian female deity Ninkasi (the namesake of Ninkasi Brewing of Eugene, Oregon) appears on a clay tablet alongside a beer recipe from almost four thousand years ago. Similar associations between women and ancient brewing have been found across the globe, from Africa and the Middle East to Central America, where a Spanish bishop in the sixteenth century recorded Indigenous women creating beerlike fermented beverages from coca pods.[52]

As the drink we would recognize today as beer took form in Europe during the Middle Ages, brewing as a so-called alewife remained an important occupation (and even a financial lifeline) for many women. But European brewing traditions in Northern and Central Europe shifted quickly after the bubonic plague swept through the continent in the 1300s, away from cottage brewers and monastic communities and toward larger-scale producers. Beer made specifically to be sold outside the home, and the rise of male-dominated brewing guilds focused on producing it, meant that fewer and fewer women were able to brew beer for sale. More perniciously, in some parts of Europe alewives became associated with witchcraft and misogynistic stereotypes. By the 1500s, the number of women in Europe's brewing industry had declined. Yet despite these efforts to exclude and threaten them, a noteworthy number of women kept working as commercial brewers. References to the ongoing presence of women brewers can even be found in Shakespeare, who in his 1590s play *Two Gentlemen of Verona* offers the line, "She brews good ale, and thereof comes the proverb, Blessing of your heart, you brew good ale."[53]

Unlike the folks back in the Isles, early British colonists in the Americas didn't have access to large-scale industrial beer production or the guilds that closely guarded brewing expertise, so women in the colonies who wanted to brew didn't face the same discrimination they'd endured in Europe. Mary Lisle became America's first recorded "brewster"—a term denoting brewers who were women—when she took over her father's Philadelphia brewhouse in 1734. But it's almost certain that other women were already operating large-scale operations throughout the colonies; they just weren't as thoroughly documented.[54]

By the time breweries started opening in Colorado in the 1850s and early 1860s, industrial lager production and the knowledge of how to craft the quaffable beverage were firmly rooted in the male social sphere among the guilds and tradesmen. Male laborers were the ones doing the brewing as the state's economy got off the ground, meaning women were locked out of Colorado's brewing industry from the outset. For this reason, the shifting expectations that ushered women out of the industry in Europe and the eastern United States didn't so much sweep through Colorado as they were foundational to a beer culture that was male-oriented from the start.

Heading into the twentieth century, any brewer with full kettles was most likely one of the bigger, wealthier operators who could employ lots of men, could afford to invest in new technologies, and had easy access to Colorado's growing rail network. Steam-powered machinery allowed brewers to increase production to levels that had been unimaginable before industrialization. Pasteurization—a technique for preserving foods that had been perfected in the 1880s—made long-range shipping without spoilage possible. The 1892 invention of the so-called crown cap to seal bottles made it feasible to efficiently package large quantities of pasteurized beer for shipment. And expanding transportation networks—especially the railroad lines that now traversed the remote expanses of the West—made it easier for brewers to develop long-armed distribution systems.

Colorado beer was able to take advantage of these advances in industrialization right away, but that didn't mean the Centennial State was

Amid Colorado's first age of brewery mergers, John Good formed the Tivoli-Union Brewery in 1901. The brewhouse operated until 1969, later becoming part of the Auraria Higher Education Center. It now houses the renewed Tivoli Brewing Company and acts as a working classroom for students in fermentation sciences programs at Metropolitan State University of Denver. *Courtesy of Denver Public Library.*

entirely freed from the constraints that had always hampered long-distance beer distribution. The beer these nineteenth-century brewers made was a living beverage that, especially before modern preservation techniques grew widespread, required constant temperature control to prevent spoilage. Partly because their beer had to be consumed near the place where it was brewed and partly owing to the transience of boom-and-bust economies during the gold and silver rushes, brewers fanned out across the state. In a pattern that would repeat itself more than a century later, small breweries popped up in nearly every mountain town across Colorado. Brewers like Jacob Mack in Aspen, John Gaster in Granite, Otto Tubbs in Pueblo, and Herman Meyer in Lake City made beer—often lager and each using his own unique recipe—that was consumed in saloons within a few miles of where it was made. Most of these breweries were boom-and-bust operations themselves, with very few staying open for more than a few years. Even fewer survived the economic disaster that was the Silver Crash of 1893, when the federal government's withdrawal of support for silver prices sent Colorado's economy into a brief but severe depression.[55]

Industrialized brewing allowed the larger brewers on the Front Range—particularly Zang's, Tivoli-Union, and Neef Brothers in Denver along with Coors in Golden—to ship their beer farther away, proffering stiff competition to smaller breweries. By the same token, out-of-state (and out-of-the-States) breweries started shipping their product into Colorado. The British-made Bass Ale became a common presence in the state in the early 1870s, and by the end of the decade, domestic brewers were following the intrepid English brewer's lead. Anheuser-Busch was shipping its Budweiser lager to Colorado by the late 1870s, and by 1900, other national brewers like Schlitz, Blatz, and Pabst from Milwaukee had joined Anheuser-Busch in distributing in Colorado, brewing one of every four beers Coloradans enjoyed.[56]

To compete with these invading national breweries, and following a pattern that was transforming other large industries at the turn of the century, the bigger Colorado breweries consolidated and sought outside capital in order to grow and leverage economies of scale. One of Colorado's most famous breweries was born of such a marriage of economic necessity. After the owners of the Milwaukee Brewery in Denver defaulted on a loan they'd taken out to finance an expansion, brewer-turned-lender John Good repossessed it, and in 1899, the Colorado brewing pioneer became a brewery owner once more. He renamed the brewery the Tivoli and in 1901 merged it with the Union Brewery, establishing the Tivoli-Union Brewery of Denver lore.[57]

Those who didn't see good prospects in consolidating looked for capital to expand their operations and keep a competitive edge. British capital had played an important role in financing railroad expansions after the Civil War and in Colorado's mining industry after 1870, but by the late 1880s, investors were looking for new opportunities.[58] As the reach of American breweries lengthened and their production continued to soar, they looked like an attractive prospect. A wave of American brewery stock offerings met with success in London in 1888 and '89, whetting British appetites. British capitalists would, in short order, hold sizable and often controlling stakes in flour milling, cattle ranching, agricultural land companies, irrigation companies (including the High Line Canal, which ran through Denver), oil operations, and a variety of other enterprises.[59]

In addition to their growth potential, breweries were especially attractive to investors because the industry offered the prospect of vertical integration and monopoly. In the Gilded Age of corporate trusts, British investors saw an opportunity to control not only the brewers' manufacturing processes but also their agricultural markets and distribution systems, a scheme that would allow them to dictate prices—and, thus, profits—at every stage. Acting on what seemed like the opportunity of a lifetime, British investors bought breweries across the United States in the late 1880s and the 1890s. In 1889, an investment syndicate based in London purchased a consolidated package of Denver Brewing Company and Ph. Zang's. That same year, eighteen St. Louis breweries were merged under the auspices of another investment syndicate, and similar financing arrangements appeared in Detroit, Baltimore, Philadelphia, and elsewhere.[60]

In a routine that may sound familiar to today's beer aficionados, this perceived foreign incursion into Colorado's brewing industry provoked a backlash among drinkers who liked to think of their local as, well, *local*. Adolph Zang, who'd inherited his brewery from his father, Philip, was forced to defensively highlight the brewery's ongoing benefits to the local economy through a series of newspaper articles that appeared around the state. Meanwhile, Adolph Coors gleefully reminded disgruntled Zang's drinkers that *his* family-owned brewery was "No Syndicate, No Company, No Trust" and that "You Patronize Home Industry When You Drink It." Likewise, the San Luis Brewery in Del Norte advertised that its beer was "made from barley grown in the San Luis Valley" and encouraged Coloradans to "Patronize Home Industry and Drink Pure Beer" rather than the presumably compromised brews made with outside barley and foreign money.[61]

Adolph Coors had become one of the state's biggest brewers by 1900, the date of this illustration. Industrial breweries like his were pumping out thousands of barrels of beer every year. *History Colorado Collection, 2003.130.1.*

From a peak of twenty-three in early 1893, the number of Colorado breweries declined to sixteen in 1895 in the wake of the Silver Crash and sank to only six in 1915 as Prohibition settled in on the state.[62] But this market contraction did not reflect a shrinking taste for beer. Based on how much product brewers were generating in the state, Coloradans were drinking 15 to 20 gallons of beer per person in the late 1870s,[63] nearly all of which was made locally. By 1910, the first time statisticians attempted to divine the actual numbers on a state level, consumption had grown to about 23 gallons per person, of which roughly one quarter was produced outside of Colorado. These estimates were per capita, meaning they included men, women, and children equally in the calculation, but of course it was (mostly) the men who doing the drinking. These habits put Coloradans as a whole slightly (but not embarrassingly) above the national average, estimated in 1912 to be between 20 and 21 gallons per person. Even thirsty Denver, where the beer consumption amounted to 43.4 gallons per person, compared modestly with New York City, which sloshed in at 76.88 gallons per person in 1910.[64]

The brewing industry's arrival, even though it wasn't heralded by the clomp of Clydesdales or the proud pronouncements of a mythical founding brewer named Adolph, was a symbol of an entirely new relationship between the people and the landscape in Colorado. Native North American economies, and the people and animals that sustained them, were violently and callously swept away to make room for Euro-American settlements and their market economies, giving rise to injustices that in many ways have yet to be fully understood or reckoned with even now more than 150 years later.

The industrialization, foreign investment, and new technologies transplanted to Colorado by those Euro-American settlers brought both challenge and opportunity. As the gold and silver rushes were drawing to a close, fossil fuels from the mountains powered an economic transition that would make Colorado the industrial capital of the Rocky Mountain West. Brewers, just like other entrepreneurs, found that new technologies and Gilded Age capital allowed them to churn out more of their product than ever before and sell it in markets that had been unreachable a generation earlier.

But trouble was looming on the horizon. Consolidation, economic strife, and rising concerns over the social cost of drinking took a steady toll on breweries in Colorado. And with Prohibition sentiment on the rise across the nation, beer and other alcohol were increasingly cast as the source of Colorado's ills.

SECOND ROUND

DRY TIMES IN THE CENTENNIAL STATE, 1916–1933

John Hanson (no relation to the coauthor) was greeted with cheers from his fellow detainees when Denver cops deposited him in the bullpen of the city jail on January 1, 1916. He'd been picked up downtown at Sixteenth and Market Streets for drunkenness.[65]

That wasn't so unusual for a Saturday in a city well known by then for its raucous saloons. What made Hanson's arrest noteworthy was that—as of midnight—Coloradans were supposed to be quite sober. Hanson had earned the newsworthy honor of being the first drunkard picked up in Denver after Prohibition became the law of the land in Colorado. And his hero's welcome reportedly included a prime spot in the cell where he could sleep it off.

Jailbirds weren't the only ones applauding that day. Colorado's cadre of anti-alcohol reformers was surely celebrating (soberly) as well. Their victory was hard won through force of conviction and grinding effort. Statewide prohibition was on the ballot a number of times prior to 1916, and each time, campaigners failed to expand the ban from dry cities like Fruita, Fort Collins, Greeley, and Boulder to the rest of the state. It was only through on-the-ground political organizing, zealous appeals to religious values, and determined campaigning that the "drys" (as prohibition advocates were known) finally got Colorado voters to ban booze in 1916, doing so four years before the rest of the country followed suit in 1920 with the Eighteenth Amendment.

Prohibition campaign button from about 1913. Legislative proposals to ban booze in Colorado were common, but few gained enough public support before prohibition came to Colorado in 1916. *History Colorado Collection, 81.90.9.*

Commercial alcohol had been illegal for just over four months on May 7, 1916, when this barrel was seized and poured into the gutter in the town of Ouray. *History Colorado Collection, 86.296.5333.*

A century later, it seems incredible that a state boasting more than four hundred breweries (and counting!) helped lead the way toward a booze ban. But looking backward in time through the lens of a pint glass reveals a misunderstood era that's often obscured by mental images of glitzy Jazz Age flappers and speakeasy spirits. In fact, those eighteen dry years were anything but carefree. They saw the rise of organized crime, the resurgence and fall of the Ku Klux Klan, the beginning of the Great Depression, and whiplash-inducing swings in the social role of alcohol. Even the flavor of American lagers today and the current craft beer boom can be explained by looking at the attitudes and habits forged during nearly two decades of Prohibition.

The dry times can seem hazy and distant, and we often overlook the historical forces that made imposing such drastic limits on personal liberty seem like a good idea. Few of us today think about Prohibition when we order our favorite pints at our local brewery or open a cold one at home. But maybe we should. After all, the results of banning alcohol can still be felt in Colorado—from the brewery to the voting booth and almost everywhere in between.

DEMON SALOONS

When the well-known New York newspaper publisher and utopian idealist Horace Greeley followed his own advice and headed west, he was shocked by what he found. Greeley envisioned the West as a wide-open landscape where liberty and opportunity would forge white men into God-fearing salt-of-the-earth farmers. They were to be the patriotic and morally upstanding backbone of America. But arriving in Denver in 1859, Greeley found a different sort of citizenry altogether: "Prone to deep drinking, soured in temper, always armed, bristling at a word, ready with the rifle, revolver or bowie knife, they give law and set fashions which, in a country where the regular administration of justice is yet a matter of prophecy, it seems difficult to overrule or disregard." With a scornful flourish, Greeley made his disappointment in the city clear to the readers of the *New York Tribune* by concluding that "there have been, during my two weeks' sojourn, more brawls, more fights, more pistol shots with criminal intent in this log city of one hundred and fifty dwellings, not three-fourths completed nor two-thirds inhabited, nor one-third fit to be, than in any community of no greater numbers on Earth."[66]

William Byers, Denver booster and publisher of the *Rocky Mountain News*, agreed with Greeley's dim view of the city's early residents. And Byers specifically pinned the source of Denver's problems on saloons and their drunken, listless patrons: "The throngs of men who line our streets and fill our concert saloons are pursued by infirmity of purpose which drives them from the active ranks of life, and makes barroom fixtures out of them who might adorn society under better circumstances."[67]

Like other journalists and public thinkers in the late nineteenth century, Greeley and Byers equated poverty, unrest, violence, and homelessness with alcohol. The saloon-going man, it was widely understood, was a victim of predatory alcohol peddlers, a breakdown of social mores, and his own lack of moral fortitude.

Such logic flourished among the cognoscenti of America's professional classes throughout the nineteenth century, propelled in part by the saloon's declining relevance to middle- and upper-class daily life. Temperance reformers across the country developed a moralizing hatred of saloons that was disproportionate to the scale of the problem they posed. One sociologist studying the "liquor problem" in turn-of-the-century Chicago concisely summarized the political aspects of anti-saloon sentiment in a speech to the city's ethics committee: "The popular conception of the saloon as a place where men and women revel in drunkenness and shame, or where the sotted beasts gather nightly at the bar, is due to exaggerated pictures, drawn by temperance lecturers and evangelists, intended to excite the imagination with a view to arousing public sentiment."[68] And arouse public sentiment they did, especially among a new generation of economic and political elites moving west in the late 1800s and early 1900s.

By the turn of the century, Denver was growing into the West's third-largest city (after San Francisco and Omaha), thanks in part to its status as a hub for rail transportation. Denver's growth helped propel Colorado into a new age of industry and prosperity, and soon rails linked mineral rush boomtowns to networks of global commerce.[69] Wealthy investors from the eastern United States and abroad eagerly sank their fortunes in building new railroads, while the smelters of Pueblo and the gold mines of Cripple Creek invited speculators from all over the world. A few became fabulously wealthy. Some local men, like Horace Tabor in Leadville, also amassed fantastic fortunes and turned their money into glittering opera houses, necessary infrastructure, and the grand, modern hotels that lured ever more wealthy residents to Colorado.

With new building came new businesses and a diversified economy. Upper- and middle-class Coloradans were soon patronizing restaurants and hotels, attending services in purpose-built churches, and voting for officials whose full-time job was public administration. In short, by the turn of the century, the wealth that came out of the ground had helped Coloradans create many of the institutions they lacked during earlier decades—institutions whose important functions had once been fulfilled by saloons.

Increasingly irrelevant to the lives of urban upper-class residents, saloons were demonized for political gain and cast (not always incorrectly) as places that lured patrons into lives of drunkenness, debauchery, and crime. While working-class Coloradans might not be collecting their mail or sleeping at the saloon anymore, they still relied on some of the services saloons provided. Wealthier Coloradans could host friends and family in their spacious Denver Squares or ornate Victorian homes in Denver's stylish Highland or Capitol Hill neighborhoods. But the row home–dwelling laborers in Auraria or the recently arrived immigrants working in Pueblo's steel sector lived in more cramped conditions. Their homes couldn't accommodate big social gatherings. Where wealthier urban dwellers had personal cooks or ate in restaurants, many working-class Coloradans still subsisted on the salty free lunches saloons gave out with the purchase of a beer.

But seen from the perspective of Progressive-era temperance advocates, the fact that saloons were pouring alcohol overrode the possibility that they served important social functions as dynamic public spaces serving an array of intensely local, on-the-ground needs for Colorado's laboring classes.

Tensions between dry factions and saloon patrons and owners stressed the already tense social fabric of far-flung mining towns across the state, where saloons had become flashpoints in simmering labor disputes. Diverse labor unions met in saloons in mining districts like Cripple Creek and Leadville, compounding the ethnic and class divisions at the heart of the debate over the saloon's place in American society. When labor disputes broke out, as they frequently did in early twentieth-century mining towns, saloons and their foreign-born patrons were often cast as the source of the poison in the well.

Nowhere was this impulse to blame saloons for labor unrest more callously on display than in a 1914 article circulated in newspapers around the state, describing the context of the Ludlow Massacre. In the article, tellingly titled "Insurrection in Colorado during the Years 1913–1914," author L.C. Paddock of Boulder came to the defense of the Colorado National Guard, which had recently caused the deaths of at least nineteen striking workers and their family members, including several children. For Paddock, the only "ruthless attack" at Ludlow was the one muckraking journalists made on the brave guardsmen who were simply standing up against anarchists "declaring loudly against the rights of property."[70] Paddock's article emphasized that Ludlow miners had met in the "29 July Saloon" adorned with "the red flags of anarchy" to "drink beer and think of blood," and he went to great lengths to shine a light on the "temper of the foreign element" in the service of proving that saloons were dens of villainy and breeders of anarchy.[71]

As the state approached the second decade of the twentieth century, saloons and the alcohol they served were being blamed for nearly every social and

Aguilar, Colorado saloon owner Fran Mazzola named his bar the 29 July Saloon in celebration of the day Italy's King Umberto was assassinated by anarchists in 1900. Mazzola flew red flags symbolizing his commitment to the international anarchist movement, and many of his patrons took part in the coal strikes that precipitated the Ludlow Massacre in 1914. *History Colorado Collection, 83.154.46.*

political problem under the bright Colorado sun. Mistrust of immigrants, labor disputes, perceptions of drinkers' low moral character, and stark class divisions all manifested in ever more strident calls to ban booze. Looking back at this time, it's tempting to take a more critical perspective on the role saloons played (or didn't) in the problems that concerned Progressive reformers. But in Colorado, as elsewhere in the country, anti-saloon sentiment was mostly born out of anxiety over social changes wrought by immigration and the Industrial Revolution. The economic division between saloon patrons and their critics hardened opinions on both sides of the saloon doors, discouraging any search for meaningful conversations or compromise.

But to paint temperance reformers uniformly as anti-immigrant xenophobic zealots is to overlook the very real problem that alcohol was beginning to pose in America, as industrialization made beer and other alcoholic beverages cheaper and more widely available than ever before.

A QUESTION OF MORAL AND PHYSICAL HEALTH

Americans in the early twentieth century drank about as much beer as we do today. After a precipitous decline in drinking rates immediately after Prohibition, beer had a long, slow recovery back to its pre-Prohibition levels. That slow rise hangs in contrast to the exponential growth of beer's popularity that had happened in the latter half of the nineteenth century. Scholars of American drinking rates, like Daniel Okrent, estimate that Americans were drinking about 36 million gallons of beer in 1850. By 1890, that figure had increased to 855 million gallons. Put another way, in those forty years, America's population almost tripled, while beer's consumption rate grew more than twenty-four-fold. By 1914, Americans were drinking about 20 gallons of beer per person.[72] This staggering rise in beer's popularity in the middle of the nineteenth century mirrors the ways immigrants reshaped America, from the saloon bar to the voting booth.

Millions of immigrants made their way to the United States in the twentieth century's opening decades, mostly from European nations where beer culture was deeply ingrained in the fabric of society. The arrival of so many men (and early immigrants were predominantly men) who knew how to make and market beer—and others for whom beer was an accepted and expected part of everyday life—propelled the libation past cider, whiskey, wine, and rum to become America's adult beverage of choice. By the twentieth century, America's love affair with suds had, in the view of temperance advocates, pushed the nation's tipplers past a tipping point. They described an epidemic of alcoholism in terms that would ring

Radical temperance crusader Carrie Nation was notorious for busting up beer barrels and saloons with a hatchet. Her "hatchetations" were motivated in part by her marriage to a drunkard. *Library of Congress, 2014685633.*

familiar to modern public health officials discussing today's tragic opioid crisis. Temperance literature focused on the ways in which substance abuse destroyed individual lives, harmed innocent children and spouses, and frayed the very fabric of society. Seen in these terms, America's drinking problem certainly must have seemed to many like a social crisis demanding a strong, far-reaching response.

A genuine and urgent sense of alarm over America's alcohol abuse spurred some drys to take drastic actions. Carrie Nation, the dry campaigner famous nationwide for hacking apart beer kegs and smashing up saloons with a hatchet, was driven to such extreme lengths in part by her first marriage to a drunkard. Nation, who was arrested for anti-saloon actions in both Trinidad, Colorado, and in Denver in 1906, was not the only woman who felt the ill effects of alcohol on her family.[73]

Throughout Colorado, newspaper articles are rife with troubling accounts of alcohol-fueled incidents of domestic violence. For example, in April 1888, the *Fort Collins Courier* reported that James Henry Howe, known around town for increasingly abusive behavior toward his wife, was lynched by an angry mob of vigilantes for murdering her while in "a state of beastly intoxication."[74] Similarly bleak accounts of violence against women perpetrated by drunken men appear in an account from Leadville, where a laborer, apparently infamous for drinking away his sorely needed wages in a saloon, was arrested in 1914 for threatening his wife and eleven hungry kids with an axe. When questioned by authorities, the besotted man gave a paltry justification for his actions: "My wife, she make me mad. She try to take my hat."[75]

Stories like these confirmed for many Coloradans the *Aspen Daily Chronicle*'s conclusion that "overdrinking amongst saloons was a dangerous public nuisance that caused many fatal encounters."[76] As anti-drinking sentiment grew, these articles increasingly took aim at saloons and beer for being just as detrimental to public health as the viral diseases that made even nondrinkers sick. Asserting a connection between alcohol consumption and pneumonia that reveals a growing tendency to view alcoholism as a public health crisis, writers in the *Rifle Reveille* warned readers in 1913, "The United States Health Service brands strong drink as the most efficient ally of pneumonia. It declares that alcohol is the handmaiden of the disease which produces ten percent of the deaths in the United States."[77] Likewise, Anti-Saloon League and Woman's Christian Temperance Union (WCTU) campaigners writing in the *Routt County Sentinel* in 1913 expressed their frustration that "[b]oards of health, armed with the police power of the state, eradicate the carriers of typhoid and quarantine, but alcohol—a thousand times more destructive to public health than typhoid fever—continues to destroy."[78]

As beer consumption rates continued their climb, temperance advocates preached to increasingly receptive audiences across the state. The town of Greeley, founded as a utopian agricultural community, was an early prohibition adopter. So was Colorado Springs. Many of Denver's suburbs—including Highland, Park Hill, and Montclair—were planned as dry communities.[79] Both Fort Collins and Boulder had saloon bans on the books ahead of the 1916 prohibition vote (drawing a sharp contrast to their present status as two of the Front Range's most hop-happy communities). Grand Junction voted for prohibition in 1909 and changed its town charter in order to break the saloon owners' grip on political power. In each of these places, drys preached about the personal and patriotic virtues of temperance to eager crowds, while progressive candidates for political office championed a platform with prohibition at its heart.

Some of the most strident advocates for reform came from Colorado's strong Woman's Christian Temperance Union chapter. Colorado's WCTU

To Make Colorado "Dry"

Patriotic RALLY

For the Home and the School!

Place ______________________

____

Date ______________________

A FAIR MINDED PRESENTATION OF THE GREATEST ISSUE BEFORE THE AMERICAN PEOPLE

Speakers ______________________

____

____

An Entertaining Hour! Good Singing!

"DRINK IS A GREATER DESTROYING FORCE THAN ALL THE OTHER PHYSICAL EVILS COMBINED."---HENRY WARD BEECHER.

LUGG PUBLISHING CO., DENVER.

This flier advertised a nonalcoholic Patriotic Rally for the Home and the School to show attendees that a good time could be had without drinking. *History Colorado Collection, 2000.11.11.*

wielded considerable influence, often flexing newfound political muscle after women won the right to vote in state elections in 1893. Led by union organizer and activist Adrianna Hungerford from 1898 to 1942, Colorado's WCTU put its weight behind reform-minded politicians like "Honest" John F. Shafroth and condemned the alcohol-fueled political machine of Denver Mayor Robert Speer.[80] During Shafroth's tenure as Colorado's governor from 1909 to 1913, Hungerford and her fellow reformers at the WCTU kept advocating for total prohibition and even got a dry referendum on the ballot in 1912.

To help spread the gospel of temperance, the WCTU opened reading rooms where former drinkers could find opportunities for sober self-improvement and a sociable alternative to the saloon. Drys also took to the streets to make known their displeasure with the soggy status quo. One "Patriotic Rally for the Home and the School" promised attendees an "Entertaining Hour" with "Good Singing!" to demonstrate that drinking was not the only way to pass the time.

Colorado's movement to ban beer picked up considerable momentum in 1914 with the outbreak of World War I. The United States was at war with Germany, and even the saloon-going residents of beer-loving Denver started to look on beer—and the predominantly German men who made it—with deep suspicion. Anti-German sentiment was on the rise, and brewers' belated efforts to market beer as a safer, more wholesome alternative to hard liquor increasingly went unheard.

From immigration and labor disputes to the state's low moral character and the disease of alcoholism, prohibition, it seemed, could be a panacea for the problems confronting the state.

HOMEBREW'S FIRST RETURN

Colorado's breweries were as dry as the state's Rocky Mountain air on the first day of 1916, and most of the population dutifully filed out of saloons and stopped imbibing. Law-abiding citizens accustomed to making the saloon a part of their everyday routines reorganized their activities to replace drinking with new social outings like trips to the movies. Temperance reformers were initially buoyed, as local churches and voluntary associations like the Benevolent and Protective Order of Elks replaced saloons as the most important sites of social organization. For Adrianna Hungerford and her fellow drys at the Woman's Christian Temperance Union, the statewide liquor ban was the ultimate victory. The state, now clean and sober, could face the world with optimism for its residents' moral and physical health.

But what about the sizable minority of Coloradans who voted *against* Prohibition? The vote was extremely close. Drys barely carried the day with their 129,589 votes (52 percent of the total) against the 118,017 votes (nearly 48 percent) from "wets"—a narrow victory of only about 11,500 votes. With all of Colorado's breweries prohibited from selling their product, thirsty beer fans had a choice: turn to nonalcoholic malt tonics and "near beer" or start making their own.[81]

Before Prohibition, alcohol-free malt tonics colloquially called near beer were marketed and sold as health drinks by druggists in pharmacies. With full-strength beer newly outlawed, several Colorado breweries ramped up their production of malt tonic due to an initial demand and profitability.[82] But for many who choose to drink, beer's buzz is an integral part of the experience,

Coors, like other brewing companies, tried to diversify its product line to keep the company alive during Prohibition. This advertisement for its malted milk product appeared along the rail line running through the brewery, seen here with the Coors family mansion in the background on the left. *Denver Public Library Special Collections, X-10045.*

and drinkers and brewers quickly decided that there was no substitute for the real deal. Many Colorado breweries—Coors, Tivoli-Union, and Ph. Zang's among them—rode out the first few years of state prohibition making near beer but soon either shut down or, like Coors, diversified their product lines to stay afloat. The Golden brewery started making malted milk and high-quality porcelain to keep its workers employed.

But despite brewers' best efforts to offer legal alternatives, Coloradans who wanted a real beer were left with no alternative but to make it at home.

Homebrewing was a viable option for thirsty and industrious Coloradans during state and national Prohibition since, in perhaps the most effective encouragement of homebrewing ever codified, the legislators who wrote Colorado's prohibition amendment initially declined to outlaw alcohol possession in private residences. Wealthy Coloradans such as Spencer Penrose—founder of the extravagant Broadmoor hotel in Colorado Springs—took advantage of this loophole by stockpiling cellars of booze that they hoped would carry them through prohibition. But those with lesser means had to brew their own prohibition potions.

Notable among them was a man named J.L. Williams of the Mount Harris coal camp west of Steamboat Springs, who started brewing in his kitchen in 1917. When state enforcement officers came around to check out his operation, they didn't dispute his right to brew, but Williams's production of a barrel per day struck them as suspicious. The agents arrested him on charges that, according to the *Steamboat Pilot*, he "was making more beer than he could possibly drink himself, even with his acknowledged abnormal capacity, and he had been selling to others of the coal camp." Williams protested his innocence and claimed that he drank all he brewed, but his case illustrates the brazenness with which Coloradans flouted the new laws when beer was on the line.[83]

Speakeasies, the homespun saloons that loom so large in our imaginations as glitzy underground nightclubs, popped up in nearly every town almost immediately following Prohibition. But few served beer, since, just like in saloon days, distilled liquor was more profitable per bottle and easier to transport—not to mention simpler to hide from the cops. In contrast to the way beer was *consumed* in saloon days, Prohibition-era beer became a beverage that people mostly made and drank at home. Denver boasted its fair share of homebrewers, and stories suggest that homebrewing was a widespread hobby around the state.

Even Denver's famed composer and jazz musician George Morrison Sr. got in on the action. Recalling his years growing up during Prohibition in Denver's Five Points neighborhood, his son George Morrison Jr. told us, "Dad made home brew. Once during the night when [noted dancer and actor] Bill 'Bojangles' Robinson was visiting us, beer started exploding in the cellar. It was a common occurrence, so it amused the family when Bojangles woke everyone up yelling, 'What's that, what's that!?!'"[84]

Aspiring homebrewers didn't need to be sophisticated in the brewer's arts to create drinkable beer. National beer retailers like Blatz, Schlitz, Budweiser, Miller, and Pabst all lent homebrewers a helping hand by selling some version of malt syrup—the glutinous product that contains all of the sugars needed for fermentation—in drugstores throughout the nation. Marketed as a sweetener for baked goods, much of the malt syrup sold during Prohibition was hop-flavored, surely leading some honest-minded shoppers and government officials to wonder who exactly was consuming all of this bittersweet bread. By 1926, Anheuser-Busch was doing a bang-up business selling more than 6 million pounds of malt extract every year, prompting brewery chairman August Busch Jr. to tell an interviewer that his company "ended up as the biggest bootlegging supply house in the United States."[85]

As any modern homebrewer will tell you, making beer with malt syrup or malt extract is a pretty simple process: stirring the sticky, sweet syrup into a pot of boiling water and adding a bittering agent like hops and some yeast is about all you need to do to create a brew that's reasonably close to what the professionals make. And if the professionals aren't making anything, then homebrew made from malt extract tastes all that much better. During Prohibition, police tended to overlook small homebrewing operations, and courts were hesitant to penalize those who used malt syrup for something other than its supposedly intended purpose. A Chicago man voiced the operating premise of many of his fellow scofflaw homebrewers when he explained, "Maybe the police wouldn't like it so much if we had a still, but who cares if we make a little beer for our own use?"[86]

For Denverites, that analysis proved sound. Denver's district attorney, John Rush, indicated at the outset of national Prohibition that he was uninterested in tracking down and prosecuting thousands of homebrewers, saying, "This is not a detective agency."[87] So much beer flowed at home during the "noble experiment" that in 1933 August Busch Jr. declared, with a tinge of jealousy, "[h]ome-brewing has been the great indoor sport in millions of American homes since 1920."[88]

Busch's sentiment affirmed the age-old truism that when Americans can't buy professionally made beer, they tend to figure out how to make it on their own.

MOONSHINE AND MOBSTERS

Despite the ease and popularity of making beer at home, the fact remains that most of the alcohol consumed during Prohibition packed more bang for the buck—wine and, especially, liquor. Americans who could afford to pay bootleggers' prices looked to illegally imported bottles from Canada or Mexico and supported a clandestine web of moonshiners throughout the dry years. For those with more modest budgets but lacking the inclination to make beer at home, spirits were the best choice, as they were more widely available and much cheaper to obtain than illegally imported beer. Spirits were easily bought in Colorado thanks in part to organized criminal outfits for whom Prohibition provided a lucrative source of revenue.

Italian American immigrants were some of the first (although we're by no means the only ones) to coordinate organized bootlegging in the state. Up until 1916, the shadowy criminal organization known as the Black Hand (Mano Nera) had little presence in Colorado. Criminals acting on their own or Italian immigrants familiar with the very real threat of organized crime in the old country sometimes used drawings of black hands as scary graffiti or as a sort of bogeyman to back up bogus threats. Those who had endured personal slights or professional setbacks sometimes invoked the mystique and fear-inspiring reputation of the Black Hand to underscore the seriousness of threatening letters written in retaliation. But organized crime was still rare in Colorado before Prohibition, and those few real mobsters who operated in the state mostly concentrated their efforts on small-time gambling and extortion rackets.[89]

As the state went dry, however, those would-be gangsters recognized that the public's desire for alcohol hadn't subsided. They also recognized that because booze was illegal, thirsty people would be willing to pay more to get it. At first, most of the alcohol trafficked in Colorado was wine—a vital part of many cultural and religious lives and not something that recent immigrants to America wanted to give up in spite of the ban.[90] But moonshine and illegally imported liquor quickly became the most popular of scofflaw spirits. Enterprising bootleggers in the southern Colorado coal country municipalities of Pueblo and Trinidad started making and secreting away their supplies, with tunnels underneath Smelter Hill in Pueblo allegedly making a particularly popular hiding spot. As Prohibition expanded to the rest of the nation, illegal distilling operations exploded (sometimes literally) throughout the state. Many of these operations were run by the nascent mob. Two families in particular—the Dannas and the Carlinos—vied to dominate the liquor trade.[91]

With many thousands of dollars in ill-gotten revenue on the line, the struggle quickly turned violent. Deadly shootouts in the streets came with grotesque results. Several met grisly fates at the business ends of sawed-off shotguns. The bloodshed finally subsided after the Carlinos defeated the Dannas, driving the rival family out of the liquor business. After establishing control over southern Colorado's bootlegging trade, the Carlinos turned their attention to Denver, where Giuseppe "Joseph" P. Roma stood atop a hard-won bootlegging empire.

Roma had worked for the Carlino brothers on his arrival in Colorado from Brooklyn in 1915, but he broke away from the Pueblo-based crime family to run bootlegging operations in the capital city. He survived the violence of Prohibition and built an empire based on bringing illegal booze into Denver. But even the end of Prohibition couldn't save him from the violence: Roma himself was murdered in his North Denver home in 1933, making way for Clyde and Checkers Smaldone—two of Roma's associates—to become Denver's most infamous mobsters.[92] The Smaldones' influence endured through Prohibition and well into the postwar era, although today many Denverites know the family for Gaetano's, their still-operating Italian restaurant in the city's Highland neighborhood.

The battles between the Dannas, Carlinos, and Joe Roma's gang led some to wonder whether the goal of banning alcohol—to cut down on the perceived violence and lawlessness of the saloon days—was even possible.

Clever criminals seemed always to be one step ahead of the law, and especially in the early days of Prohibition, they took advantage of a woefully underprepared law enforcement system.

Colorado in the early twentieth century had no statewide law enforcement agency. Residents feared that such forces would be a threat to the life and liberty of even law-abiding citizens.[93] Although the 1916 Prohibition law provided for the commission of special officers known as "Prohibition Executive Agents," there were nowhere near enough of them to cover all of Colorado's 104,185 square miles. Thus, responsibility for pursuing and apprehending offenders often fell to municipal officers or county sheriffs, whose authority to enforce the law ended at the town or county line. Colorado bootleggers quickly became aware of these jurisdictional boundaries. If pursued by the local cops, they would use their new automobiles—often bought with moonshine money—to scoot across county lines and wait for the heat to die down before proceeding with their deliveries.

Partly in response to the exploding bootlegging activity, Colorado upped the size and authority of its police force in 1921 by commissioning the Colorado Rangers. Returned veterans of World War I manned this full-time professional force, wearing their old army uniforms with wartime insignia removed. Their charge was to support local law enforcement efforts. Rangers joined in raids on gambling dens, speakeasies, and moonshining

The officer on the far right is Eddie Bell—the only Colorado Ranger to be killed in the line of duty, in 1922. Bell's partner said that the two of them were beaten and robbed at a gas station in Limon, Colorado, in retaliation for their work against local bootleggers. *Courtesy of John McFarlane.*

operations—places where the perpetrators were likely to be gathered in large numbers or heavily armed, or both.[94] Although most law enforcement officers did their best to stem the flow of illegal booze around the state, there was too much demand and too much money to be made from bootlegging and moonshining to stop the scofflaws. Corruption and bribes greased many palms, and police often looked the other way.

Despite the high demand for booze, Coloradans of all stripes quickly got fed up with what certainly was a major increase in crime. Denver in particular was the site of some impressively brazen incidents of lawlessness. When no arrests were made after a home belonging to a member of the Carlino family exploded violently in 1931, the *Denver Post* voiced the frustration many Denverites felt with their police by remarking that it would be great if Denver Chief of Police Robert F. "Diamond Dick" Reed and his department could "catch something besides a cold."[95] Desperately seeking safety and security in their communities, pro-dry Coloradans—particularly those white Anglo-Protestants who helped usher in Prohibition—were willing to support anyone who promised them a solution to rising crime.

In the first half of the 1920s, that solution, for an alarming number of Coloradans, came in the form of the Ku Klux Klan.

PROHIBITION AND THE RISE OF THE KU KLUX KLAN

By the time the rest of the nation went dry in 1920, the Ku Klux Klan had already targeted the city of Denver for expansion, looking to lodge itself firmly within the state's most important political offices. During the dry decade, Denver Mayor Benjamin F. Stapleton was a well-known and prominent member of the Klan, as was his chief of police, William J. Candlish. Judges and city officials statewide eagerly joined the Klan, as did countless police officers.[96]

Using political influence rather than outright violence as their primary tool of intimidation, by the mid-1920s Colorado's KKK controlled policy in much of the state. As it grew, the Klan found eager recruits, especially in communities still struggling to integrate immigrants and to control the flow of illegal alcohol; respect for law and order became the Klan's rallying cry. Much of the virulent nativism and racism Colorado's KKK espoused in the early 1920s was tied to those new immigrants, whom one Las Animas County judge characterized as "foreigners, who by education and training believe in the use of intoxicating liquors."[97]

In few places did this double-barreled anti-immigrant and anti-alcohol message find a more receptive audience than in Pueblo. After enduring shocking violence over control of the liquor trade, the city's considerable population of Anglo-Protestant residents welcomed the Klan and its promise to clean up the city. The KKK's public debut in Pueblo came in 1923 with a series of induction rallies. In June of that year, an estimated 3,200 Klan members from up and down the Front Range gathered in a field north of

THE DEFENDER OF THE 18TH AMENDMENT

Colorado's Klansmen positioned themselves as a vigilante Prohibition enforcement gang to help legitimize their discriminatory and xenophobic agenda. Under the guise of aiding the police to bust bootleggers and fight crime, the Ku Klux Klan sent the message that anyone who wasn't white and Protestant was unwelcome in Colorado. *History Colorado Collection.*

town to induct 200 new members into the Pueblo "Klavern" (the KKK's term for local Klan cells). The scene repeated itself again in September with several hundred more members swearing fealty to the KKK and joining together to burn crosses, eat barbecue, and sing hymns.[98]

The Pueblo Klavern undertook one of its first actions in February 1924 in response to a grand jury's finding that the police department was either inept or corrupt, but either way hadn't done enough to enforce Prohibition in Pueblo. With about fifty Klan members backing him up, Klansman and County Sheriff Samuel Thomas led a series of liquor raids in South Pueblo. Going from house to house, Klansmen searched the homes of Latino and Italian residents for illicit booze or the means to make it. Despite ruining quite a lot of people's evenings, Thomas only made seven arrests, and almost all of those searched and arrested were recent immigrants to the state. The message the Klan meant to send was clear: white Anglo-Protestants were fed up with Hispano and foreign-born Prohibition scofflaws, and they were willing to take enforcement into their own hands if the police couldn't handle the job.[99]

White supremacy and anti-immigrant xenophobia remained major platform planks for the Klan in Colorado as Klaverns solidified their footholds in southern Colorado throughout 1924. By continually reminding residents of the link between bootleggers and immigrants, the Klan veiled their racist intentions behind a veneer of patriotic vigilantism. In Walsenburg, south of Pueblo, 350 Klansmen paraded silently through the streets on a chilly January morning bearing American flags and banners with slogans like "The Bootlegger Must GO" and "America for Americans." The *Walsenburg World* newspaper reported that cheers and enthusiastic applause met the Klansmen all along their parade route, underscoring just how influential the KKK had become in Colorado.[100] Klaverns appeared in Trinidad and other southern Colorado towns, each holding similar rallies and preying on fear of immigrants and pent-up frustration with the local police department's feckless response to bootlegging.

This exasperation was also acute in the state capital. As the biggest city and the state's financial and political center, Denver was another regional hub for the liquor trade, making it a ripe target for Klan organizing. Speakeasies dotted the city, and mob families like Joe Roma's gang controlled Denver's flow of booze from an Italian enclave on the city's north side. Despite help from a dedicated but undermanned corps of Prohibition agents, special police, and Colorado Rangers, Denver cops were just as helpless as those in Pueblo at stamping out bootlegging and stemming the violence that went along with the sale of illegal booze. Residents of the Queen City of the Plains experienced a 28 percent jump in the crime rate between 1919 and 1920, and the tide of illegal activity kept rising; the short-lived *Denver Express* newspaper reported on the unprecedented "wave of lawlessness sweeping Denver" in 1921.[101] Prohibition violations accounted for most of the increase. In fact, Americans' disregard for dry laws was so widespread that the term *scofflaw* entered the lexicon specifically to describe it.[102]

Even when the cops did sweep up the odd scofflaw in their dragnet-style Prohibition busts, prosecutors were hesitant to bring charges against drinkers and juries were equally hesitant to convict. Much to the annoyance of many local residents, Prohibition lawbreakers walked free more often than not. Making matters worse was a pervasive knowledge that Denver's police department was rife with corruption. Many police officers were indeed on the take, and bribery was common practice with officers often willing to look the other way when mobsters came around handing out rolls of cash.[103] Corruption was so extensive that Denver's district attorney was quoted in the *Denver Post* as saying, "The present city administration is a disgrace to American government."[104] Just like elsewhere in Colorado, the situation proved ripe for exploitation by the KKK.

Arriving in Denver in the spring of 1921, organizers for the Atlanta-based Klan found fertile ground among men of the city's population fed up with rising crime. Aiding these men and women (Colorado had a particularly strong women's Ku Klux Klan presence) on the ground and protecting the Denver Klavern from the city's anti-Klan response was a job eagerly filled by a local physician named John Galen Locke. Born in New York in 1873, Locke moved to Colorado in the early twentieth century. He had a checkered medical career in Denver and was never admitted to either the Denver or the Colorado Medical Society, likely owing to his belief in the power of homeopathy over conventional medical practice. But whatever Locke's failings as a physician, he was a charismatic leader with a genius for effective organization—traits he would employ to extend the Denver Klavern's control over state and local government.

The women of the Klan, led by Imperial Commander Laurena Senter, were just as vehement in their xenophobia and racism as their male counterparts. They were recruited at first from the ranks of the wives, daughters, and sisters of Klansmen, and their messages centered on protecting true womanhood from what they saw as the denigrating influences of immigrants, people of color, and non-Protestant Christians. Cloaked in the rhetoric of upholding civic virtue and Protestant values (which she viewed as one and the same),

Senter traveled around Colorado conducting initiations and overseeing recruitment for the state's eleven thousand female KKK members organized into as many as thirty-five chapters. Hooded women held rallies, burned crosses, and preached their hateful messages about the corrupting influence of intoxicating liquors, even organizing a boycott of Denver department store Neusteters because it was run by Jews and spoke out publicly against the Klan.[105]

For the men and women of the Klan, the first opportunity to grab the levers of political control came during the mayoral election of 1923. Running as a Democrat, Benjamin F. Stapleton beat incumbent Dewey Bailey with broad support from important institutions like the *Denver Post*, as well as powerful individuals like his personal friend Galen Locke. Despite his well-known affiliation with the KKK, Stapleton was swept into office after running on promises to tackle bootlegging and root out corruption in the city government. Upon taking office, Stapleton appointed Klan members to fill positions at all levels until nearly every department was well stocked with Klansmen. Notably, he initially refused to appoint a Klan member to lead his police department, fearing (correctly, as it would turn out) that mixing the Klan and the leadership of the police would bring about disastrous results for Denver's residents, not to mention his own political image.[106]

By 1924, the chorus of Denverites questioning Stapleton's integrity was growing, and city residents initiated a recall campaign explicitly motivated by their mayor's obvious entanglement with the Klan. Stapleton was forced to wholeheartedly embrace the Klan and its aims in order to defeat the recall. Locke needed to be appeased as well, so to show his gratitude for the Klan's staunch support (and its members' $15,000 campaign donation), Stapleton appointed William Candlish as the new chief of police. Candlish had no police experience and no qualifications other than his Klan connections. His appointment was certainly connected to Stapleton's campaign pledge to "work with the Klan and for the Klan in the coming election" and to "give the Klan the kind of administration it wants."[107]

Thanks to Locke's political organizing, Stapleton won his recall election. After celebrating its victory by burning a cross atop South Table Mountain in Golden that was so large the fire was visible fifteen miles away in Denver, the Klavern acted with even more impunity. With William Candlish (who gained the nickname "Koka-Kola-Kandlish" for his overt displays of his Klan connections) at its head, the Denver Police Department turned into one of the primary vehicles by which the Klan executed its agenda of intimidation. Protestant officers were asked to become Klan members, and those who did were, in the words of historian Robert Alan Goldberg, "rewarded with choice assignments, shorter hours, and promotions. The rest joined Jewish and Catholic police officers working night shifts on undesirable beats."[108]

At Candlish's direction, these new Klan members within the police department concentrated on Prohibition enforcement efforts in Denver's Black, Jewish, and Italian neighborhoods. Enjoying total immunity from any oversight by, or repercussions from, the Stapleton administration, Denver police initiated a widespread campaign of terror and repression in the guise of enforcing Prohibition. Officers cited obscure and semi-forgotten laws as they terrorized and intimidated Jewish and Catholic shop owners who carried government-permitted sacramental wines. In Five Points, Denver's historically Black community, Klan-affiliated police used speakeasy raids as their preferred tool of intimidation. All across the city and the state, Klan-driven Prohibition enforcement became an excuse for sending an unmistakable message: unless you are white and Protestant, you are not welcome here.[109]

The Klan reached the height of its influence in Colorado after winning several statewide offices, including the governorship, in 1924, and the organization's white supremacist agenda looked to be on track to dominate Colorado politics for the rest of the decade. But mastering the means of obtaining power wasn't the same as exercising it. As the decade wore on, Klan-backed politicians found that Prohibition enforcement was a less appealing message when it was coming from a group with such obviously antidemocratic and discriminatory aims. As a result, Klan support ebbed in the latter half of the '20s, and by the time Prohibition was repealed in 1933, Colorado's male Klan had all but dissolved. (The WKKK persisted under a new name, still led by Laurena Senter, until the mid-1940s.) Stapleton distanced himself from his hooded patrons, and Locke was forced out of the Klan for embezzling funds, eventually landing in jail for tax evasion.

Although the Ku Klux Klan's political dominance ultimately proved to be a flash in the pan, its use of Prohibition enforcement as a guise for more sinister discriminatory action was an effective political move that helped legitimize the more odious planks of its hateful platform.

BEER LEADS THE WAY BACK

Beer flowed freely again, all across the country, on December 5, 1933, with the official ratification of the Twenty-First Amendment. A lot had changed in the fourteen years' time that alcohol was illegal at the national level, and in many ways, the nation that clamored for repeal was not the same one that had lobbied for Prohibition.

Much of the change in sentiment was a result of the Great Depression. Beginning with the Wall Street crash of 1929 and lasting throughout the '30s, the Depression fundamentally reordered social and financial priorities in American homes and in the halls of Congress. Throughout Prohibition, badly needed tax revenues from liquor sales weren't collected. Instead, those dollars were shunted into bootleggers' pockets. The cost of enforcing Prohibition compounded the revenue problem for Depression-era governments at every level, and as the hard times wore on, the bare hypocrisy of Prohibition shone through more clearly as voters saw enforcement efforts focused on poorer communities while the rich were largely allowed to consume without consequence.

So, by 1933, with the Great Depression sowing despair and Prohibition's failure to deliver on its promises being out in full view, many more Americans were thinking that they could really use a drink.

Beer led the way back. Brewers and pro-repeal groups argued that beer was neither as intoxicating nor as dangerous as liquor or wine, and they successfully lobbied the government to classify low-alcohol beer as "non-intoxicating." This expedient got beer flowing and people back to work as quickly as possible because it exempted weak beer from federal Prohibition laws. Brewers were therefore able to deliver beer that was 3.2 percent alcohol by volume without waiting for full repeal, and on April 7, 1933, legal beer was again for sale in the United States.

The Cullen-Harrison Act (which brought low-alcohol beer back) filled in the gap until the Twenty-First Amendment could be ratified by the states. Weak beer went on sale throughout the summer and fall of 1933, but liquor and stronger beer sales waited for Utah to provide the deciding vote ratifying the Twenty-First Amendment on December 5. (Colorado had voiced its approval in September.) Even with the full return to legality on the federal level, the states would need to rewrite their own alcohol laws—all of which the Eighteenth Amendment had nullified in 1920. In Colorado, legislators argued with one another through that first week of April 1933 about whether to grant municipalities a "local option"—laws that would allow specific towns to stay dry and enforce a ban on even low-alcohol beer. Lawmakers in support of self-determination at the community level prevailed, leaving cities across Colorado—including Fort Collins, Greeley, and Boulder—to continue to enforce Prohibition within their limits as the rest of the state embraced repeal.[110]

But those across Colorado who'd hoped to welcome beer back with a late-night cold one were disappointed, and most who bid farewell to legal beer in 1916 with unsatisfying lemonade toasts may have found themselves welcoming repeal in the same manner. As the *Rocky Mountain News* reported, "Hotels are planning no beer party celebrations for tonight. Whatever celebrating is done, has been left entirely to individuals in Denver—and there is little likelihood many of them can obtain the beer for such a celebration before tomorrow night at the earliest." One reporter covering the non-event in an article headlined "Beer Becomes Legal Here but City Sleeps Thru It" noted, "You couldn't hear a quaffing sound any place."[111]

The brewers at Coors and the Tivoli-Union—the only two breweries in Colorado ready to ship their product on April 7—discouraged a boisterous welcome back. They feared that raucous parties might give voters second thoughts about the consequences of repeal. Indeed, committed prohibitionists clung to hopes that legal beer would either slake the nation's thirst or prompt enough bad behavior that it would horrify lawmakers into realizing their mistake and put a halt to the full repeal campaign. But the brewers refused to play into their hands. "'We're not in favor of any national holidays,' said one brewer [to a reporter from Denver's *Rocky Mountain News*].

'We plan to conduct a decent, respectable merchandising business and we will start the sale of our product on that basis.'"[112]

When the taps finally started flowing the next day, "the rush to sample the beer exceeded the expectations of the most enthusiastic sponsors of the beverage." Supplies quickly ran low in the face of overwhelming demand, but revelers remained on their best behavior. The *News* reported that whereas Denver had been averaging three to ten arrests per night for drinking during the waning days of Prohibition, there were "no arrests, auto accidents, or disturbances of any kind" as Denverites welcomed legal beer back. "In fact," the reporter concluded, "from the standpoint of sobriety and arrests, the day was one of the queerest encountered by police in years." The open presence of women at the celebrations added to the strangeness of that day for some, since co-mingled public drinking would have been uncommon before Prohibition. In a dramatic demonstration of just how many changes Prohibition had wrought, Denver's servers reported that "women were among the enthusiastic samplers of the beverage in its initial day." The paper even ran a photo of smiling, well-dressed women raising a stein right alongside the men to prove it.[113]

Immediately after repeal, the most visible change in Colorado's beer landscape was the absence of saloons, which never regained their central role in community social life. Even those who'd worked hardest to defeat Prohibition did not intend to welcome the saloon back to its former place in American life. Pauline Sabin, enemy of prohibition and leader of the Women's Organization for National Prohibition Reform, made it clear to reporters in 1933 that she was in no way advocating for a return to pre-Prohibition ways: "'I can't conceive of the old saloon being allowed to come back,' she said. 'Of course, if you mean by a saloon a place where liquor is bought and consumed, it will come back, but there will be improved conditions.'"[114]

Brewers took her point (or perhaps her warning) and, in place of the saloon, began promoting the home as the proper setting for enjoying a cold one. Once again using a suite of technological advances to transform the industry, the brewers took advantage of the widespread adoption of refrigerators and radios during the 1920s and '30s to rebrand beer. The vinyl-coated, or "keg-lined," steel beer can, introduced in 1935, was another catalyst for transitioning drinking into the home. Cans were less expensive for brewers to produce and easier to transport than bottles, and they were easier for consumers to store in the fridge. In-home mechanical refrigerators had been a rare luxury at the beginning of Prohibition, but by 1933 they were in a full quarter of American households—allowing more Americans to grab a cold one in the kitchen with unprecedented ease.[115]

The trick for brewers was actually getting consumers to buy their beer at the grocery or liquor store. To do so, marketers focused on convincing middle-class women (who they assumed did the shopping for their household and who'd been the moral force of the temperance movement) to view beer as a household staple and an important component of the American Dream rather than a threat to their family. Keeping the fridge stocked for the men in their lives would, advertisers suggested, keep those men from heading out to drink in bars and would thus promote domestic happiness. As radios became common conveniences through the 1920s and '30s, marketers found that sponsoring programs geared toward housewives was an effective way to convince women to buy their product.[116]

The brewers' message took hold. Whereas 90 percent of beer before Prohibition had been packaged in kegs destined for saloon taps, by 1935 about one-third of all beer was shipping in cans and bottles. By 1940, nearly half of all beer came in packaging meant for home consumption. Once they'd convinced women (or so they imagined) to stock the fridge with beer, brewers wanted those women and other nontraditional beer drinkers to enjoy it as well. To appeal to a wider range of palates, some of those brewers lightened their lagers by tamping down the "beer flavor" and lowering the alcohol content. They reduced the amount of malt in their recipes and mixed in additives with milder flavors, such as corn and rice. They cut the hops back to a minimum. The result was a style of American lager that was, and is, easy to drink—and unlikely to prompt the kind of uncouth behavior that was associated with pre-Prohibition saloons.[117]

Changes in the way it was made and marketed reflected a brand-new understanding of beer's place in society. Co-ed drinking was a rarity in Colorado before 1920, but the necessarily underground nature of alcohol consumption during Prohibition, when mixed with the shifting social norms of the Roaring Twenties, enabled men and women to drink together in public establishments. With repeal came a more relaxed attitude toward beer consumption, and advertisers across the nation encouraged this change by positioning beer as the perfect accompaniment to every household event. By 1933, not only had beer become a backyard beverage, it had also morphed into a basic element of life in America—something women and men consumed together in the comfort of their suburban homes.

In Colorado, where the twin wallops of the Dust Bowl and the Great Depression nearly wiped out the state's economy, a great many started thinking of beer as a commodity that brought comfort, jobs, and a sense of community back to a population navigating its way into an uncertain future. Its subsequent popularity in the state (and even our contemporary craft beer boom) have their roots in the beer culture that emerged after nearly two decades of Prohibition.

In Colorado, those eighteen years saw the end of the saloon era, the rise of organized crime, women winning the right to vote in national elections, the beginning of the Great Depression, the rise and fall of the state's Ku Klux Klan, and a radical shift in the social role of alcohol. These tumultuous times not only reoriented Colorado's relationship with beer, they also completely reset the state's relationship to alcohol as a whole. Everything from the social settings in which it was consumed to the way it was made to the laws that governed its production and consumption was different after Prohibition.

The dry years left behind a bare patch of soil from which Colorado would have to regrow its beer industry—literally from the ground up, one barley field at a time.

THIRD ROUND

COORS COUNTRY, 1933–1979[118]

The city of Golden bubbled with activity day and night through the first week of April 1933. The Coors brewery—where Prohibition had prevented the company from brewing anything stronger than malted milk since 1916—was once again making its "fine light beer." Locomotives delivered loads of empty bottles (more than 750,000 that week alone), while 125 men worked around the clock in badly needed Great Depression–era jobs.

At one minute past midnight on Friday, April 7, a special train pulling twenty-one refrigerated cars chugged out of the brewery with more than eighteen thousand cases of Coors beer destined for thirsty cities across Colorado. At the same time, a fleet of more than seventy fully loaded delivery trucks drove out of the brewery gates. A patrol from the Jefferson County Sheriff's Office met them, and more were stationed along the route to keep roads clear and to protect the shipments from anyone tempted to theft.[119] After almost eighteen years of illegality, beer was once again available to residents of the Centennial State. Or at least to those who could get their hands on one of the coveted cases.

Of the state's forty-four pre-Prohibition breweries, only four survived the dry times. And only Coors continued making beer through the rest of the twentieth century. Trinidad's P.H. Schneider struggled on under several different names and owners until the brewery doors shut for good in 1957. Tivoli-Union in Denver darkened its canning line in 1969, marking the (fortunately temporary) end of the second-oldest continuously operating brewery in the United States. And the beloved-by-many Walter Brewing Company in Pueblo turned off its brew kettles in 1975 (although the brand has since been revived).

As its competitors fell away, Coors continued to thrive. Throughout the late twentieth century, its marketing and the mystique born of its rarity outside the seven states where it was sold made Coors beer practically synonymous with the Rocky Mountain West. By the 2000s, Coors was near the top of its popularity, regularly beating offerings from much bigger brewers like Budweiser and Miller. Even with the dawning of the age of craft beer, Coors maintained its mystique and enjoyed a massive sales lead over even the biggest and most popular of Colorado's craft competitors.

Its path to prominence was bumpy. It survived Prohibition, strikes, scandals, and divisive politics to come out on top. Like it or not, Coors is the Golden brewery with the Midas touch, and its story is *the* story of Colorado beer in the twentieth century.

TASTE THE HIGH COUNTRY

American palates shifted lighter after Prohibition. The kaleidoscope of flavors and styles Coloradans enjoyed in the early 1900s was largely extinguished by almost twenty years of illegality, leaving behind only the most popular pre-Prohibition style beers: pilsner-style lager.

Always known for its light flavor, Adolph Coors's pilsner-style beer was exactly what Americans were looking for. Light, drinkable, and not too bitter, Coors Banquet Beer appealed to a nation of aspiring drinkers who'd lost their taste for the dark, roasty malts of stout and the bitter twang of hop-heavy pale ales. In fact, all across the country, the vast majority of the beers being poured after Prohibition were lighter lagers. Coors outpaced the industry by decades when it released a lower-alcohol and lower-calorie version of its flagship called Coors Light Beer in 1941. Despite a successful launch, rationing during World War II forced Coors to discontinue its light brand, which would not reappear until 1978.[120]

Even through the 1950s, the Coors family had never done much advertising for their product, relying mostly on consumer demand and an expanding population throughout the West to drive expansion. Whereas the nation's other industrial brewers devoted up to three dollars of the cost of every barrel they made to marketing, Coors only spent around seventy cents per barrel.[121] Anheuser-Busch, Schlitz, Miller, and Pabst grew their distribution networks to become national brands that shipped beer from coast to coast, but Coors focused on selling its beer in only a select number of western states. While most American brewers were using pasteurization

Left: Young Adolph Coors was one of many German immigrants who arrived in Colorado in the late 1800s, bringing their beer and beer culture to the state. *Courtesy of the Coors Archive.*

Opposite: This 1936 ad was one of the few marketing materials from the brewery that established a long Coors marketing tradition of convincing customers that the natural splendor of the Colorado high country made the company's beer special. *Courtesy of the Coors Archive.*

to make their beers shelf-stable and chemical agents to age them, Coors relied on old-fashioned methods.[122] As competitors filled the market with a variety of lighter beers designed to satisfy lighter tastes, Coors abandoned styles like light, bock, and amber lagers in order to focus on its flagship original recipe.

In these ways, Coors set itself apart from other large regional breweries dominating the post-Prohibition market and bucked the trends that transformed the brewing landscape all around it. The family-run brewery in Golden was selling all of the beer it could make and didn't bother worrying about things like market share or competition from brewers with larger distribution networks. According to company lore, the quality of its crisp light lager and a robust regional network of distributors kept sales strong, and for almost a century, the Coors family found success in doing what they had always done: brewing a "fine light beer." By the late 1950s, Coors was the top seller in the eleven states west of the Mississippi in which it was distributed.[123]

Brewery chairman Bill Coors—a trained engineer and the third generation of the Coors family to run the company—reinvested in the beer's quality after becoming chairman in 1959. To ensure that the product delivered the experience consumers had come to expect, Coors developed a cold-filtering process as an alternative to pasteurization that kept the beer chilled and sterile rather than subjecting it to flavor-damaging heat. Cold-filtering, the company said, allowed customers to bring home keg-quality beer—something that was impossible with pasteurized beers. But cold-filtering came at a price. It meant that Coors beer needed to be continually refrigerated from brewery to backyard barbecue, a fact that

Coors Golden Export Lager is as clean, as pure, as fresh as the crystal clear Rocky Mountain water used exclusively in its brewing—which gushes from an eternal spring on the Coors property at the foot of Lookout Mountain in Golden, Colorado.

Brewery Chairman Bill Coors helped pioneer seven-ounce aluminum beer cans in 1959. It was the nation's first large-scale aluminum beer canning operation. *Donated to the Denver Public Library by the* Rocky Mountain News.

layered logistical constraints on the company's existing predilection to keep distribution close to home.[124]

Cold-filtering (and, depending on who you asked, the taste of the beer itself) distinguished Coors from its competition during the 1960s and enhanced the company's reputation for putting product quality above expanding sales.

By the late 1970s, Coors had become somewhat of a legend. It had grown into the fourth-largest brewery in America, even though its beer was still sold (legally) in only thirteen states.[125] Luminaries throughout the 1970s, from actor Paul Newman to President Gerald Ford, were known to raise a glass, and the *New York Times* observed that Coors had "won a reputation as the elixir of beers, the brew of Presidents, a prize to be smuggled into the East." The author of one popular treatise on beer at the time gushed that "Coors has gone all the way for quality.…[It] must be handled almost

By the 1940s, Coors had invested in a fleet of refrigerated trucks to ensure that its unpasteurized beer stayed cold and fresh from brewery to backyard. *Denver Public Library Special Collections, X-10018.*

like milk." *TIME* magazine called it the "Chateau Haut-Brion of American Beers," putting it on a footing with France's most legendary wines. Even Hollywood offered a cinematic toast to Coors's mystique with *Smokey and the Bandit*, a 1977 box office hit that chronicled Burt Reynolds's highway hijinks as he bootlegged a truckload of Coors from Texas (the farthest east it was legally sold) to Georgia, winning a bet and Sally Field's heart in the process. Off screen, bootleg cases of the brewery's classic Banquet Beer smuggled to the East Coast in the early '70s fetched as much as $15 (equivalent to more than $100 today) for beer that was often spoiled in the process by poor climate control.[126]

Even in 1978 as Coors began, slowly and sometimes reluctantly, to expand its marketing budget and its distribution outside the West, it held on to its Rocky Mountain mystique. For at least fifty years, the company traded on the mythic purity and beauty of the place where it was made with the slogan "brewed with Rocky Mountain spring water." Although many brewers touted their water as what set them apart from others, Coors advertising leaned heavily on Colorado's snowy high-country reputation to show consumers what made its beer different. In one of the company's early forays into the world of television marketing, an advertisement from the 1950s describes how the purity of snowmelt from Colorado's granite peaks accumulates in tiny crystal pools—the water's purity is echoed in the "clean, refreshing taste of Coors—a product of the high country."[127]

Subsequent advertising spanning more than five decades repeatedly drew a connection between the beauty of the Rocky Mountains' scenery and the quality of Coors beer. The messaging stuck, and as Coors expanded its distribution reach and its marketing budget, the idea that Colorado was a special place with special beer went out across the nation—branding not just the beer as special, but the Centennial State along with it.

"This is the reason there is only one Coors brewery in the world," actor Mark Harmon explained to the nation's television watchers in 1985 as he hiked along a snowy creek near Guanella Pass in the mountains southwest of Denver. Ducking under a snow-laden branch, Harmon got to the point: "When this snow melts, it'll flow through miles of porous rock and sand. This natural filtration helps create a clarity, a purity that's so remarkable, Coors doesn't have to do a thing to their water. Rocky Mountain spring water. Helps give Coors a difference worth tasting." Commercials like this one made it clear that the allure of scarcity, the sheen of celebrity endorsements, and the beer's fine, light flavor weren't the only things that made Coors popular with its customers. As the company more fully embraced advertising in the late 1970s, it continued relying on this association, linking its beer to Colorado's extraordinary landscapes and the West's ideals of rugged individualism.

And Colorado was a good brand to be associated with in the '70s and '80s. As John Denver's ode to the "Rocky Mountain High" topped the charts in 1972 and '73, the state experienced its biggest spike in population growth since the decades of gold and silver rushes a century before. Many of the new residents came for the benefits of living in the Rocky Mountains—the starry skies John Denver sang about on the radio and the snow-clad peaks Mark Harmon extolled on television. By portraying Coors as a uniquely Colorado product, memorable advertisements added to the mystique surrounding Coors by reinforcing the notion that the beer was special because of its place of origin. And it didn't hurt that commercials featuring Harmon hiking in the snow or pulling a Coors out of a crystal-clear mountain lake also encouraged beer drinkers to bring a cold can of Coors along when they headed outside to enjoy the West's natural beauty.

CASH FOR CANS

More than simply cheering outdoor recreation, Coors also heralded the era's growing environmental ethos by developing the beverage industry's first aluminum cans. Searching for an alternative to steel cans, which were expensive and liable to produce off-flavors in beer, Coors debuted one of the nation's first aluminum beverage containers in 1959. The new two-piece aluminum cans sealed better than the three-piece steel cans brewers used throughout the early twentieth century, so the new cans better protected the beer's flavor. As a bonus, aluminum's infinite recyclability meant that if the brewery collected enough used cans, it could stop buying aluminum slugs and start manufacturing its own from recycled materials. Recycling would cut costs and allow the company to simultaneously boost its image by instituting a can buy-back program—a public relations perk touted as a design element that the *Denver Post* later called a "salvage feature aimed at cutting down litter."[128]

Cutting down litter was important, as empty beer cans had become such a common sight along the nation's highways and in otherwise scenic places that they were often invoked as a symbol of America's wasteful consumer culture. In Colorado, caretakers at mountain parks along the Front Range complained of the piles of empties left behind by outdoor partygoers, while residents of mountain towns like Steamboat Springs worried that beer cans and other trash along the road would hurt tourism. The state's chief highway engineer even lamented how much time maintenance crews wasted repairing flat tires popped by shrapnel when their mowers ran over yet another can.[129]

Beer cans were such a symbol of the litter problem that a popular 1961 book about the issue was titled *The Beer Can by the Highway: Essays on What's American About America*. The author, John A. Kouwenhoven, drew national attention to the litter problem and particularly to the beer can's contribution to mounting garbage, arguing that discarded beer cans were emblematic of a society with so much material wealth that consumers didn't give a second thought to the problem of waste. The book tapped into a growing number of Americans' fears about a polluted planet, concerns that were propelling the American environmental movement toward political prominence.[130]

Bill Coors acknowledged the bad optics of so many cans—often with his family's name on them—littering otherwise pristine-looking western places, some of them places he may have enjoyed visiting himself. "Beer cans along the highways, in the parks and at picnic grounds have become a major public relations problem for the brewing industry," he explained to Denver's *Rocky Mountain News* as early as 1955. "We think the answer may lie in returnable aluminum cans," he continued, outlining the company's efforts to develop a better beer can.[131] When the company introduced the aluminum beer can in 1959, news reports relayed the company's hope that the can's recyclability—and the incentive of a penny per can to those returning them—"will help reduce litter on highways and picnic grounds."[132]

That hope was quickly realized. By 1965, Coors was boasting that in the years since the aluminum can's introduction, it had brought home 60 million empties after consumers had enjoyed their contents, including 12.5 million the previous year. In Colorado and Wyoming, the heart of Coors Country, more than 85 percent of the company's cans were being returned. "For our part we regard it as an investment in preserving the native beauty of our country," a company spokesperson told the *Rocky Mountain News*. "We're proud you seldom find a Coors aluminum can along the roadside or marring the approaches to a trout stream."[133]

In 1970, as more and more brewers and other beverage makers adopted Coors's aluminum can design, the company expanded its recycling efforts. Coors launched a "Cash for Cans" program that paid consumers to return their used aluminum cans regardless of who'd made them, giving consumers an incentive beyond environmentalism to stop tossing empties to the side of the road. Speaking to the *News* in January 1970, Bill Coors explained that "[a]luminum is the best possible answer to litter because it is salvageable." Not only that, but by recycling aluminum rather than buying new supplies, the company could save hundreds of thousands of dollars each year on the cost of raw materials. Through the Cash for Cans program, and the parallel

Coors launched a buyback program for its cans in 1959. Later, the brewery built its own can manufacturing plant that used recycled aluminum from the cans it collected. That canning business became part of the Ball Corporation, today one of the nation's largest aluminum can manufacturers. *Courtesy of the Coors Archive.*

program it established to recycle glass a year later, Coors was able to further reduce the amount of aluminum and glass it had to buy from suppliers while simultaneously addressing the litter problem its throwaway packaging had exacerbated. In large part thanks to Coors's efforts, by 1985 Colorado led the nation in aluminum can recycling.[134]

Touting the company's eco-leadership, Coors bolstered its bottom line and its brand at the same time, ensuring its appeal to a growing segment of the middle class who were falling in love with the outdoors and who were justifiably concerned about their ecological legacies. Coors's strong identity as a uniquely Colorado company fit well with this environmental ethos. By the same token, Coors advertising showcased an appealing version of the Rocky Mountain lifestyle and cultivated a western cachet that helped establish Colorado's brand throughout the country during the second half of the twentieth century.

The contours of the state we know today—with its fabled outdoor recreation industry and brewing scene—echo the Colorado that appeared on television and the radio thanks to Coors (and John Denver) in the

1960s and '70s. With state and federal investment in highways providing unprecedented access to alpine amenities and new markets for Coors beer, it was easier than ever to enjoy a taste of the Rockies. A half-million people liked the flavor so much that they decided to move here in the 1960s and '70s, increasing the state's population by 25 percent in just ten years. By the 1980s, the word was out: Colorado was a great place to live—and drink beer—and Americans flocked to Coors Country en masse.[135]

BEER IN THE 'BURBS

As Americans greeted the decades of optimism and prosperity that followed years of economic depression and, ultimately, victory in World War II, pent-up demand for new housing and cars fueled suburban construction booms across the United States. For millions of Americans—especially military veterans supported by the GI Bill, government mortgage programs, and other financial benefits that were unavailable for Black veterans—the American dream of homeownership was suddenly within reach. But where railroad and streetcar lines had shaped growing cities in earlier generations, highways drove postwar growth—literally. The mobility that cheap, long-range automobiles gave families allowed them to buy homes far from the city center, fueling demand for single-family dwellings. It was the golden age of American suburbs, and they blossomed all across the country.[136]

In Colorado, much of the economic growth underpinning suburban expansion was fueled by federal government spending geared toward countering the perceived threat of Communism during the Cold War. Particularly along the Front Range, the U.S. government expanded military installations like the Fort Carson Army Base in Colorado Springs, the Pueblo Ordnance Depot, and the Rocky Mountain Arsenal near Denver. The feds built facilities like the Air Force Academy and the Air Defense Command in Colorado Springs, the Rocky Flats nuclear plant between Golden and Boulder, and the Federal Center in Lakewood (on the site of the old Denver Ordnance Plant). Scientific labs were established near Boulder, including the National Center for Atmospheric Research and a branch of the National Bureau of

Standards. These agencies took advantage of the brainpower concentrated nearby at the University of Colorado, which also enjoyed growing federal research funds. In all, federal defense and research spending accounted for more than 20 percent of Colorado's revenue between 1952 and 1962—a figure amplified by the arrival of defense and technology companies and federally funded projects like the construction of Interstates 25 and 70.[137]

Colorado's population surged in step with all of this federal investment, and good-paying jobs weren't the only thing bringing people here. A growing appreciation of the state's natural amenities enticed a rush of new residents in those Cold War decades. In the twenty years between 1950 and 1970, the number of Coloradans grew from 1.3 million to 2.2 million, with most of them settling near Denver. New suburbs emerged or expanded as folks found their own slice of the American Dream in the vast tracts of single-family homes built in towns with names like Lakewood, Westminster, and Littleton. These suburbs added nearly 560,000 new residents in that time, while the population of Denver proper grew by fewer than 100,000—a demographic shift that fundamentally reshaped the character of Colorado's Front Range.[138]

Around the region, the story was the same. Towns on every side of Denver expanded dramatically, while a growing network of highways linked them into an interconnected metropolitan area.[139] When the Denver-Boulder Turnpike opened in 1952, Boulder was a sleepy university town of just over 20,000 residents, including the students. By 1970, that highway had linked it into the burgeoning metro area, and Boulder's population more than tripled to 66,870. Nearly 14,000 travelers every day paid the twenty-five-cent toll to go back and forth on US-36 between Denver and Boulder. Suburbs like Martin Acres appeared on the south side of town, closest to the turnpike, offering three- and four-bedroom homes with around one thousand square feet for about $13,000.[140]

As people in Colorado and throughout the country headed out to the 'burbs, beer followed them home. In 1945, a trade group of brewers calling themselves the United States Brewers Foundation launched an advertising campaign aimed at depicting the ways "Beer Belongs" at home. Between 1945 and 1956, the "Beer Belongs" series (also known as "Home Life in America") created at least 136 advertisements featuring Americans enjoying beer in a variety of familiar settings like backyard barbecues, family gatherings, game day parties, and vacation spots.

Created by some of the top commercial artists and illustrators of the day, the spots ran in such popular magazines as *Time*, the *Saturday Evening Post*, *Collier's*, *U.S. News*, and more. Each idyllic vignette featured middle-class men

"BACKYARD BARBECUE" by Stevan Dohanos. Number 4 in the series, "Home Life in America," by noted American illustrators.

Beer belongs...enjoy it

In this home-loving land of ours . . . in this America of kindliness, of friendship, of good-humored tolerance . . . perhaps no beverages are more "at home" on more occasions than good American beer and ale.

For beer is the kind of beverage Americans like. It belongs—to pleasant living, to good fellowship, to sensible moderation. And our right to enjoy it, this too belongs—to our own American heritage of personal freedom.

AMERICA'S BEVERAGE OF MODERATION

Left: Ads like this one sent the message that beer was an integral part of American life and fit into the wholesome family-oriented domestic ideal of the time. *Courtesy of the Beer Institute.*

Opposite: Between 1945 and 1956, the "Beer Belongs" series (also known as "Home Life in America") featured more than 100 advertisements showing Americans enjoying beer in a variety of familiar settings. *Courtesy of the Beer Institute.*

and women enjoying leisure time and beers together, with most depicting smiling groups of friends and family—and, notably, almost always equal numbers of men and women. Every ad insisted that "Beer Belongs," often explaining, "In this friendly, freedom-loving land of ours—beer belongs… enjoy it!" Many also reminded viewers, emphatically, that beer is "America's Beverage of Moderation."

Ads with lengthier copy extolled beer's role in the good life at home in America:

> *In this home-loving land of ours…in this America of kindliness, of friendship, of good-humored tolerance…perhaps no beverages are more "at home" on more occasions than good American beer and ale.*
>
> *For beer and ale are the kind of beverages Americans like. They belong—to pleasant living, to good fellowship, to sensible moderation. And our right to enjoy it, this too belongs—to our own American heritage of personal freedom.*

Themes of domesticity, freedom, and patriotism were especially resonant in the Cold War era, and the strategy worked spectacularly. In 1940, fewer than half of American families had been in the habit of bringing beer home to drink. But by 1950—five years into the "Beer Belongs" campaign—the Brewer's Foundation was celebrating that the share had risen to two-thirds of the nation's households. And in beer's new domestic setting, women were loving it right along with men. By 1954, the Brewer's Foundation could report that four in ten women nationwide drank beer, accounting for 22 percent of the beverage's consumers.[141] The basic strategies and trends established after Prohibition's repeal carried forward and got amplified through the 1950s, '60s, and '70s as sales of bottles and cans climbed to 80 percent of all beer.[142]

But people of color were notably absent from the "Beer Belongs" ads. Out of about 160 unique advertisements, not one features a person of color. The unmistakable message was that even though non-white people may be able to buy beer, the American Dream that went along with it would remain out of reach. Housing discrimination was written into new neighborhood covenants and city ordinances as the suburbs continued their growth outward from Denver, marking an era of white flight, when many white families left the city center, that persisted past the civil rights era. Whether intentional or not, the decision brewers made to market their beer to an audience of white Americans reflected very real racial tensions that would come to a head in the 1960s and '70s.

As Colorado entered the latter half of the twentieth century, its white residents were riding high on what felt like an unprecedented wave of optimism and prosperity in comfortable suburban homes. People of color may not have been so lucky; for many in Colorado's non-white communities, beer ads were yet another reminder of the discrimination they faced in choosing where to live and work.

Even as beer was held up as a great way to celebrate living the good life, it had also become another symbol of the ways the American Dream was not an option for so many Coloradans.

"CHICANOS, STOP BUYING COORS!"

Coors may have been a darling of the beer world in the '60s and '70s, but not everybody was in love.

In the late 1960s, activists in Colorado's Chicano civil rights movement, known as El Movimiento, were calling for a boycott of Coors to protest unfair hiring and promotion practices at the brewery. Labor unions, gay and lesbian rights groups, the NAACP, and other civil rights organizations in Colorado and around the nation joined in, all citing unfair or discriminatory treatment. Pressure on the brewery built through three decades, and by the 1990s, ongoing skirmishes with unions and a change in the brewery's leadership had brought about a major shift in company policies that mirrored a broader reorientation of the relationship between consumers and companies everywhere. With social consciousness on the rise and in vogue in the era's push to expand civil rights to all Americans, consumers took to voting with their wallets—making clear that they expected to see companies commit to supporting equity. Corporations large and small found themselves subjected to boycotts over charges of discriminatory labor policies. And some of those boycotts, like the one targeting Coors, would live on for decades.

The protests of the 1960s and '70s were by no means the first time Coors had found itself at the center of controversy. Notoriously unfriendly to the cause of organized labor, the Coors Brewing Company had long tangled with strikers: what was an initially irksome labor dispute over worker pay grew into a full-blown strike in 1890 when the company initially refused to meet its workers' demands. Crisis was averted and workers got back on the production line the next day after the company grudgingly agreed to a thirty-cent raise and a guaranteed ten-hour workday.[143] But the specter of labor unrest had risen, and it loomed over the Golden brewery for the next half century.

Negotiations with workers devolved into strikes with some regularity over the years, and the brewery's management grew increasingly impatient with each disruption. "For years we have been harassed by the union," Grover C. Coors remarked in 1916 to the *Colorado Transcript*, summarizing his family's early frustrations with organized labor. And their antipathy to organized labor endured. Speaking to the Master Brewers Association in 1978, Bill Coors apparently made an explicit connection between labor and the great bogeyman of the era, socialism: "I'm not saying organized labor is itself socialist, but it's a force pushing things into socialism."[144]

A young boy joining the boycott movement against Coors. The company was accused of racially discriminatory hiring and promotion practices, and that legacy lives on for some Coloradans who cannot forgive the family or the company. *Photo by Juan Espinosa, History Colorado Collection, 2016.87.35.*

Historians of the company regard the dry years as a watershed moment for the Coors family in that it crystallized the dangers of government regulation and organized labor to their industry's survival. For Adolph Coors Sr., a German immigrant whose life story reads like a parable for the bootstrap spirit of the American entrepreneur, striking laborers were lazy ingrates who wanted something for nothing—disloyal to the company and unappreciative of the benefits the Coors family provided its workers.[145] Following Prohibition's repeal and the return to beer sales, the Coors family, and Joe Coors in particular, took on a personal role in ensuring that the government would be restrained in its power to take away the family's livelihood and that unions would never again threaten the brewery's bottom line.

After a botched kidnapping tragically took the life of Adolph Coors III in 1960, his brother Bill took over day-to-day management at the brewery. With Bill Coors focused on maintaining quality and rolling out his new aluminum cans, Joe Coors waded into the nation's increasingly fractious politics just as the civil rights movement of the 1960s was reorienting everything. Racial divisions—for so long the central question at the heart of American politics—were reset with the Civil Rights Act's passage in 1964. Communism was looming across the globe, as was rising sentiment against the war in Vietnam. Suddenly, reliably Democratic states turned Republican as the GOP became a haven for those who saw the Civil Rights Act as turning the country in an uncomfortable direction and antiwar protestors as Communist sympathizers.

This political reorientation took hold fast as a grassroots movement, but business leaders who argued that governments at all levels had amassed too much power gave it further momentum. By the 1970s, America's political system had almost completely turned on its head. The Republican Party took the lead in promoting conservative values, while Democrats—historically more aligned with conservative social and economic values and racist policies like Jim Crow laws—embraced racial equality and liberal fiscal policies. Contemporaries and historians dubbed these parties the "New Right" and the "New Left" for the ground each broke in order to form new coalitions and new consensus around the problems that were manifesting across the nation.

For Joe Coors, a believer in the values expressed by the New Right, the threat of Communism and a sense that government regulations were strangling American entrepreneurs set him in motion. When a seat on the University of Colorado's Board of Regents opened up in 1966, he threw his hat in the ring. His campaign focused on combating Communism, which he argued was on the rise within the university's left-leaning academic community, and ensuring that conservative voices were not being sidelined at CU. Joe won the seat the next year and quickly moved to enact anti-Communist policies such as mandating that faculty take loyalty oaths. But his fellow regents and some of the faculty weren't so eager to take such a forceful stand; they complained to the press when he used his position to "propagandize right-wing extremism" by distributing anti–United Nations materials from the John Birch Society, a conservative organization that advocated strict limitations on government.[146]

The following year, Joe Coors played a leading role in banning the influential Students for a Democratic Society (SDS) organizing group from campus and brought a rising conservative luminary, California's Governor Ronald Reagan, to speak.[147] Taking on an ever more prominent role in the conservative movement—both in Colorado and on the national stage—Joe became something of a figurehead for the social flashpoints of his home state after a fiery commencement address he gave to graduates of the Colorado School of Mines in 1969. To a surprised audience, he allegedly railed against welfare recipients, hippies, and the "pleasure-loving parasites" who are "satisfied to live off the state dole and handouts in a carefree existence."[148]

Still, Joe Coors's tenure as regent lasted six years, and it proved a springboard for his growing political consciousness. The contacts he established as regent—most notably a personal and financial relationship with soon-to-be President Reagan—lent him a megaphone with which he would advance his political philosophy within state politics. And Joe certainly found receptive audiences for his messaging in Colorado, a state where the majority of voters were dependably conservative. But his last name was Coors, and with the brewery's rising prominence in the beer industry, it was clear that the Coors family and its brewing company were getting pulled into a fight over the state's political future.

Among those gearing up to offer a competing political and social vision were brewery workers from the Latino community who confronted discriminatory hiring and promotion practices long in place at Coors. Around the same time that Joe Coors was standing up for the conservative social values he felt were under threat at CU, a new civil rights movement was gaining ground in Colorado. El Movimiento grew out of a rising cultural pride in Chicano identity in the 1960s and '70s, and its activists directly tackled entrenched racial discrimination against people of Latino descent across the state. In Denver, local boxing legend and poet Rodolfo "Corky" Gonzales became an outspoken leader who helped catalyze widespread protests. In 1967, Gonzales helped found the Crusade for Justice, an organization that joined the fight against discriminatory employment policies (among other injustices) by taking aim squarely at the Coors Brewing Company.[149]

Prejudice was widespread in Colorado, and Coors, like many other large companies in the state, discriminated against Latino workers by hiring them primarily for unskilled or low-paying positions. The company's workforce was overwhelmingly white and male well into the 1970s, and it only hired its first Black employee in 1962. Despite Latino workers making up about 13 percent of the local labor pool, only 2 percent of Coors's workforce came from Latino families. Discrimination was by no means something unique to Coors. But unlike less iconic Colorado companies, the Golden brewery

The Brown Berets march in Denver during the boycott against Coors in 1973. They were protesting racially biased hiring and promotion practices at the Golden brewery. *Photo by Juan Espinosa, History Colorado Collection, 2016.87.16.*

had a popular and easily recognizable brand with an outspoken leader who represented the forces that maintained the discriminatory status quo. Joining with a coalition that included local unions, the Crusade for Justice allied with groups like the GI Forum to kick off a boycott of Coors beer as a way of calling for equitable employment practices and greater opportunity for Latino workers at the Golden brewery.[150]

As the protests spread out from Denver and Golden in the late 1960s, the choice of which beer to drink became an emblem of one's political leanings. Public protests weren't limited to Golden. Forty-three students at Southern Colorado State College (today's Colorado State University Pueblo) joined hands around the campus pub to protest the sale of Coors in 1967, adding their voices to a rising chorus of statewide anti-Coors sentiment.[151] Happening against the backdrop of Cesar Chavez's California lettuce and grape worker boycotts, the Coors protests shone a national spotlight on discrimination in Colorado's businesses and on the Coors family itself. That spotlight intensified in 1977 when the American Federation of Labor and Congress of Industrial Organizations (AFL-CIO) called for its member unions to join the boycott in support of yet another labor strike at the brewery.

The Coors brewery's influence over its unions had grown through the early part of the century, and the company used a combination of generous perks and active dissuasion to erode labor organizing among its workers. Labor action was seldom successful, and strikes ended in dissolution more often than achieving concessions. In spite of all of the pressures on the company, the 1977 strike ended in a spectacular victory for Coors. The company deftly played its cards, going on a charm offensive with a spot on the TV news program *60 Minutes* while hiring strikebreakers who forced its union to vote for decertification. The upshot was that while the boycott was still in effect, the Coors Brewing Company achieved a long-standing dream: it was finally free from the ever-present aggravation of organized labor.

Although the original movement to boycott Coors officially ended in 1987 when the AFL-CIO came to an agreement with Joe Coors's son and newly minted chairman, Peter, it lives on in the hearts of many who cannot forgive the company for its initial refusal to address racially discriminatory practices. For others who still refuse to drink Coors beer, it's impossible to ignore the family's role in the rise of the New Right and in advancing a political philosophy at odds with their own. Ultimately, the long-running boycott brought no clear-cut victories to the activists, but it did tarnish the company's mystique and hurt its sales. By the late 1980s, a new generation of leadership embodied by Peter Coors (and eventually mergers with international beer brands Molson and Miller) made amends with some of the communities the company had offended. Today, Coors is noted for its corporate citizenship, particularly in its support of gay and lesbian consumers. In the early 1990s, it

Although its track record on labor and anti-discrimination policies is a history that some Coloradans can't forgive, Coors today has been recognized for its corporate citizenship. Notably, Coors was among the first major companies to offer spousal benefits to same-sex couples. *History Colorado Collection, 99.43.3.*

was among the first large American corporations to extend spousal benefits to same-sex couples.[152]

Through the social turmoil of the 1960s and '70s, the Centennial State found itself swept up in the larger political and economic currents shaping the country. The labor disputes and boycotts at Coors Brewing Company were an expression of a broader shift in the relationship between corporations and their consumers happening nationwide.

"THE FINEST BEER IN THE STATE, MADE FROM IMPORTED HOPS"

Even as sales slowed as a result of the boycott and strikes, the 1960s and '70s saw Coors Brewing Company experiencing its most significant period of growth. Brewing enough beer in Golden to satisfy the company's clamoring devotees required a large—and ever larger—amount of barley and hops. And like Colorado brewers of the past, Coors faced challenges in securing adequate, reliable supplies of those key ingredients.

In response, the company sought to ensure quality and control costs by bringing as many aspects of the brewing process as possible in-house. As Coors expanded, quality and price control through vertical integration of the brewing business would become one of the company's hallmarks.

This was particularly true of barley. Company president Bill Coors often summed up the brewery's appreciation of barley by saying that "barley is to beer as grapes are to wine. You cannot make a good wine out of bad grapes and you can't make a good beer out of bad barley. You can make a terrible beer out of good barley. That's easy to do. But at least start right."[153] For the Coors family, barley was second in importance only to the pure Rocky Mountain spring water that the company had touted in its advertisements since 1937.

Like other brewers before Prohibition, Adolph Sr. had offered seed and incentives to Colorado growers in order to ensure himself a supply of quality barley. During the 1898 planting season, he ran ads proclaiming, "I would like to see more barley raised in our country and offer nice, clean, four rowed Scotch seed barley at $1.00 per 100 lbs. I am willing to contract for No. 1, clean barley raised from this seed at $1.00 per 1000 lbs. delivered at brewery. Screenings returned. A. Coors."[154] The barley was malted in-house at the brewery, avoiding the need to buy from out-of-state distributors as his competitors sometimes did.

After Prohibition's repeal, when the big breweries increasingly outsourced their supply chains to expand capacity and cut costs, Coors, now led by Adolph Jr., doubled down on its in-house barley program. The program began in 1937, when Adolph found a small packet of seeds from that year's two-row Moravian barley crop included with an order of malt from R. Karsten Ltd. in Prague, Czechoslovakia. Coors gave the seeds to a local gardener to test their suitability to Colorado's climate. When the barley grew well, his company started working with more growers to scale up over the next few years until the crop was ready to be malted and tested in the beer. The result was good, and 1945 consumers enjoyed the first Coors lager made with locally grown barley.[155]

After this initial show of success, the brewery quickly scaled up its barley program, enhancing the vertical integration of its operations. A breeding program at the company's experimental farm—created in 1949 in the San Luis Valley—developed better high-altitude varieties from the original seed stock using Mendelian (non–genetically engineered) methods. In facilities it built beginning in the 1950s near Loveland and in Monte Vista in the San Luis Valley, the company stored barley it collected directly from farmers until it was needed at the brewery in Golden, where a large, custom-designed malthouse was completed in 1957.[156]

By the mid-1950s, the locally grown high-country barley had joined the famous Rocky Mountain spring water as another uniquely regional asset to the brand. A pamphlet prepared for barley growers touted "this climate and our certified seed strain" as the reasons for Coors's "superior malting barley." The company billed itself as "Makers of Coors, America's Fine Light Beer…Produced from Moravian Malting Barley Grown by Colorado Farmers."[157]

Although the state's first farmers to grow Coors barley were concentrated in southern Colorado's San Luis Valley and in the northwest part of the state, as demand for Coors continued to grow—and particularly with the expansion of the company's distribution area in the 1970s—the need for barley grew in concert. Coors looked to the Northern Rockies and developed growing areas with farmers in Wyoming, Idaho, and Montana. By 1971, the company had contracts with more than five hundred farmers in several Rocky Mountain states for 6 million bushels of barley, for which Coors paid

Colorado's brand was on the rise in the 1970s, and nobody did more to spread the Rocky Mountain mystique than Coors (and maybe John Denver). Advertisements like this one traded on the beauty of the place where it was brewed to mark Coors beer as unique. *Courtesy of the Coors Archive.*

$2.01 per bushel (more than $15 in today's dollars) at the elevator. The company's expansion plans called for more than doubling the harvest to 12.5 million bushels by the end of the decade.[158]

Ever since the days when Adolph Sr. offered to return "screenings"—maltster lingo for barley kernels that weren't up to his standards—the brewery had always imposed strict quality requirements on its barley growers. As the barley growing program spread regionally in the latter half of the twentieth century, Coors dictated increasingly rigorous specifications in its contracts for the barley it would accept.[159] Dealing in ever-larger scales of production amplified the need for such tough standards. A slight increase in the protein level of barley can reduce the final volume of beer it produces, and even small percentage reductions mean significant shortfalls when amplified across tens of millions of barrels of production annually.[160]

In the pursuit of higher quality and more reliable supply, the company even tried to impose stricter specs on nature in order to insulate its supply chain against crop shortfalls and price shocks. Ever the engineer, Bill Coors launched a cloud-seeding program in 1972 in the San Luis Valley in an attempt to suppress hail and optimize the weather for barley growing, thus enhancing the reliability of the grain supply. When ranchers and other valley growers balked at the thought of drier summers just to make more beer, the company threatened to terminate contracts with 20 percent of its growers each year until the valley was supplying only 10 percent (rather than 60 percent) of Coors's barley needs or until the growers could bring their fellow citizens around to a weather management program. Noting that the company had developed other options, Bill Coors explained that "10 per cent is the maximum amount we are prepared to place at the mercy of the natural elements which in our experience will give us a good quality crop once in 20 years."[161]

Valley residents never agreed to the weather modification program, but the company didn't follow through fully on Bill Coors's threat to marginalize the region. By contracting with irrigated operations, the company has mitigated some of the vagaries of the weather, and expansion in other areas has reduced the company's reliance on the San Luis Valley. But the region remains a significant producer of Coors's unique strain of Moravian two-row barley.[162]

If one strategy for controlling cost and ensuring a reliable supply of quality brewing ingredients was to integrate the supply chain into the brewery business—managing every step from seeds to suds—an alternative approach was to diminish the role of potentially temperamental ingredients.

At Coors, Rocky Mountain spring water and high-country barley were the stars, and the company went to great lengths to control its sources of those key ingredients. Hops, on the other hand, were an essential component of the supporting cast but hard for Colorado brewers to source close to home, and Coors used them with a light hand. While Adolph Sr. advertised for better barley, he ceded the territory when it came to hops. Coors ads from the same era touted its beer as "The finest Beer in the State, Made from Imported hops."[163]

The first beers brewed in Colorado had been "innocent of hops," and Coors had never strayed far from those origins. Since opening its doors in 1874, the company had prided itself on brewing an exceptionally light and refreshing lager. Whereas pre-Prohibition lager recipes had often featured more pronounced hop profiles than today's most popular American pale lagers—some popular lagers at the turn of the twentieth century had more than double or even triple the hop profile of today's Coors and Coors Light—Coors had always been notable among its competitors for its lightness.[164] There was a pragmatic business aspect to Coors's distinct light taste. What the brewers couldn't control, they wouldn't allow to control *them*. Lower hop usage reduced the company's reliance on hop suppliers in New York, the Pacific Northwest, and Europe, which Coors couldn't integrate into its operation as easily as it could barley growers.

Lighter hops also made the beer more approachable—a key consideration after Prohibition, when attracting new beer drinkers was crucial to a brewery's survival. As Bill Moomey, the company's advertising director, recalled, Adolph Coors Jr. explained the strategy behind his beer's light flavor to him in the early 1950s: "You take a young person....He wants to drink beer but he doesn't really like the taste very much because of the bitterness of the hops....We strive for lower bitterness units in part to attract that young beer drinker. Because when he then tastes one of our competitors, it will taste too bitter and he'll come back to us." In short, "We make it less unpleasant, so our beer will be easy to get on and hard to get off."[165]

For Coors, controlling every aspect of brewery operations gave the company an advantage in the postwar suburban beer boom, when uniformity of flavor and low alcohol content were in demand. Lighter beer appealed to Prohibition-era palates unaccustomed to the bitterness of hops or the toasty sweetness of malt, and it sold like gangbusters in the decades after repeal. Coors made the perfect product for the age: a backyard beer that tasted best when served as cold as the Rockies.

Coors came of age alongside its home state. As Colorado grew and transformed itself over the course of the twentieth century, Coors was along for the bumpy ride. The Coors Brewing Company stood shoulder to shoulder with Schlitz, Budweiser, and Miller—the last giants standing tall as the Era of the American Behemoth Brewer reached its zenith in the 1970s. Fine light flavor and "drinkability" paired well with Coors's high-country marketing, and Colorado's brand soared to new heights with every Banquet Beer and Silver Bullet sold.

But for a growing number of Coloradans, the glitzy ads masked growing pains. The company's star dimmed in the face of racist employment practices, labor strife, and a wide-ranging boycott. Coors became a focal point in the era's political clashes, since for some, the Coors family and their brewery stood for the regressive racial backlash against the Civil Rights Act and divisive politics of the age. Ultimately, the long-running boycott didn't produce any clear-cut victories for activists or progressives, but it did tarnish the company's mystique and hurt sales. By the late 1980s, a new generation of Coors leadership was making amends with communities it had offended and working to move past (although some would say obscure or whitewash) its controversial, discriminatory history.[166]

Coors marketing, inextricably tied as it was to its home state's reputation, deftly promoted a vision of the good life in Colorado that drinkers could capture one can at a time. As the company ramped up its marketing efforts in the 1970s, cold cans of Coors became synonymous with the things many Coloradans loved: hiking trails, ski runs, and, starting in 1995 with the inaugural games and bespoke Blue Moon beer at Coors Field, Major League Baseball.

With its malting programs and deep knowhow established by generations of brewers, Coors set the stage for Colorado's craft beer boom. Brewmaster Keith Villa, creator of Blue Moon Belgian White, recalls helping the then-tiny New Belgium Brewing Company get its yeast strain right, and even Holidaily—the tiny niche all-gluten-free brewery in Golden just a few miles up the road from Coors—sourced its own knowhow from former Coors employees who'd left the megabrewer to start their own breweries.[167]

New Terrain Brewing Company (another Golden favorite) looks out across the mesas at the site of Coors's pre-Prohibition beer garden. Dave Johnson, brewer for New Terrain, thinks about this connection as he ponders the future of beer in Colorado. For him and many of the more than four hundred craft brewers that have sprung up in the state, the association Coors forged in the 1970s between beer and time spent outside helped set the stage for the microbrew movement of the 1990s, as well as the state's strong beer industry today. The thirsty bikers and trail runners who congregate at New Terrain gather there for the same reason Coloradans flocked to the banks of Clear Creek in the late 1800s: to enjoy a refreshing beverage and cool off amid the natural beauty of Colorado's Front Range.[168]

Today, international megamergers and consolidation in the mass-market beer industry have taken most of the Coors company out of Golden. The Molson-Coors company's headquarters is now in Chicago—a midwestern city Adolph Coors Sr. saw as an oversaturated market when he chose Colorado as the place to found his brewery in 1873. The classic Coors Banquet Beer is still made only at the company's original brewery site, tucked between the dramatic mesas that define Golden, Colorado. But even with its corporate HQ far away, Coors is still synonymous with its home state, and its rocky history mirrors Colorado's own turbulent ups and downs.

Whether you're still boycotting Coors or it's your go-to drink for sipping at Coors Field, the beer's story can show us much about ourselves and how our version of Colorado came to be.

FOURTH ROUND

BREWING THE NEW WEST, 1980–TODAY[169]

In 1989, husband-and-wife brewing team Jeff Lebesch and Kim Jordan made a trip to Belgium to sample what was then the most diverse selection of beers in the world. With a knowledge of homebrewing and their mountain bikes in tow, Lebesch and Jordan took to Belgium's back roads in search of the Trappist breweries famous for creating uniquely flavorful brews. At the time, they simply wanted to find recipes and ingredients that would add depth and complexity to their homebrewed beer.

But just four years later, the pair's recently opened New Belgium Brewing Company was pumping out nearly thirty thousand barrels of ale from its Fort Collins brewery. Their beer was an unqualified hit. Thirty thousand barrels was still only about 2 percent of the volume produced by the gigantic Anheuser-Busch plant just up the road, which the megabrewer had opened in 1988. But for a microbrewer like New Belgium to capture that kind of market in just four years was an industry feat that hadn't happened in Colorado since the nineteenth century.

Belgian-inspired ales were reasonably new and unique in the early '90s but still accessible and refreshing to the average beer drinker's palate. Although there were other breweries in Colorado and even in Fort Collins—notably Odell Brewing Company and Coopersmith's Brew Pub—consumers loved New Belgium brews, and many connected with the marketing. The clever name Kim and Jeff gave their beer was "Fat Tire," in honor of the mountain bike trip that inspired the brand. It might not have been the first beer to forge a connection between outdoor recreation and craft beer, but the association resonated with consumers in a way previous attempts hadn't.

Kim Jordan and Jeff Lebesch started New Belgium Brewing Company in the basement of their Fort Collins home. In those days, each bottle of New Belgium beer came printed with the couple's home phone number. *Courtesy of New Belgium Brewing Company.*

Until 2020, when the beer behemoth Kirin bought the company, New Belgium was one of America's biggest independent craft breweries. The empire Kim Jordan and Jeff Lebesch built reaches across continents—something the pair probably weren't envisioning in 1991 when each bottle of New Belgium beer came printed with their home phone number for quality assurance calls. Since those days of hand deliveries and basement brewing, Coloradans have opened hundreds of other breweries, and a handful of those have grown into large operations with nationwide distribution networks. Their breweries—once slapdash operations—now occupy entire industrial parks.[170]

But what accounts for the fact that craft brewing took off so strongly and so early in Colorado? Why did New Belgium and so many others start here? How could the relatively small towns of Fort Collins, Boulder, and even Denver stand comfortably next to established beer cities like London, Flanders, or Munich as the best places in the world to get a pint? Was it Charlie Papazian, one of craft brewing's early and most effective evangelists, and his

cadre of homebrewing pioneers setting up the right conditions? Was it the Great American Beer Festival or the presence of Coors Brewing Company and its CEO Peter Coors's "rising tides lift all boats" ethos? Was it the Rocky Mountain spring water?

While all of these ingredients were important additions to the final mash, the short answer is that—as is so often the case in Colorado's history—the landscape drove the movement. It was the mountains and their many recreational opportunities providing the economic conditions to support what was then called "microbrewed beer." For more than a century, Americans and other settlers came west to seize the economic opportunities created by extractive industries like mining, ranching, agriculture and logging. The New Westerners who started Colorado's craft beer industry flipped that model on its head.

They came for the lifestyle and then figured out how to support themselves and their outdoor recreation habits once they'd arrived.[171]

A BRIEF HISTORY OF HOMEBREWING IN THE UNITED STATES

To understand how a small cadre of homebrewing hobbyists along Colorado's Front Range made the Centennial State what it is for beer drinkers today, it's worthwhile to survey the veritable river of homebrew running through American history.

In fact, Americans have brewed beer at home since before they called themselves Americans. While some Indigenous peoples throughout the continent produced fermented beverages with beerlike attributes, beer as we know it today arrived in the Americas with European settlers. The early English and Dutch colonists who established settlements along the eastern seaboard of what would become the United States in the seventeenth century were provisioned with beer, but their supply too often spoiled on the transatlantic voyage. To fill the void, colonists brewed in their homes as well as in their shops and taverns. When traditional brewing ingredients were unavailable, colonial brewers experimented with the ingredients on hand, concocting suitable substitutes from indigenous crops such as pumpkins, persimmons, molasses, maize, sassafras, and spruce needles (establishing a precedent of experimentation for craft brewers nearly four centuries later).[172]

Homebrewing stayed popular even as supply lines got more reliable and domestic barley and hop growers made commercial breweries viable over the next century and a half. George Washington famously brewed beer (or, rather, supervised its brewing by enslaved workers) at home in Mount Vernon, as did Thomas Jefferson (or, more accurately, Martha Jefferson, who was famous for her wheat beer) and many of their fellow colonists. The taste for experimenting (or making due) with nontraditional ingredients didn't diminish much either: Washington's 1757 "Small Beer" recipe calls for a healthy infusion of molasses, one of the Jeffersons' beers used persimmons, and a Virginian contemplating the threat of reduced British imports in 1775 published his recipe for making beer out of green cornstalks.[173]

After the Revolution, the new United States set its sights on expanding across the continent, and Americans carried their taste for beer into the West. The first recorded brewer in the trans–Mississippi West was John Collins. He was a member of the Lewis and Clark Expedition who crafted an ale for his companions out of waterlogged bread made from camas roots as the Corps slogged through Oregon on their way to the Pacific Ocean in 1805.

Expensive to transport and liable to spoil en route, however, commercially brewed beer trickled slowly westward until the gold rush brought enough thirsty men across the continent to support an industry. Throughout much of the nineteenth century, western explorers and early settlers with a taste for beer were compelled to brew their own refreshments until settlers arrived in sufficient numbers to justify the founding of a commercial brewery. Like their resourceful colonial forebears—and for the same reasons—they learned to brew beer from spruce tips and other convenient flora.[174]

As cities popped up across the West in the nineteenth century, commercially brewed beer became readily available across much of the nation, so homebrewing's popularity faded. But Prohibition's ban on professional brewing raised up a new generation of homebrewers in the 1920s and '30s. Easier than ever before, thanks to commercially made hop-flavored malt extracts from companies like Pabst and Schlitz, homebrewing enjoyed a renaissance. Basement brewers kept the tradition alive even after the dry times ended, but the hobby had to remain an underground affair since the Twenty-First Amendment declined to extend the sanction of legality to homebrewing.

Many repeal-era homebrewers believed—or at least often asserted—that a simple clerical error had been responsible for leaving homebrewing out of the Prohibition repeal legislation that had restored other modes of alcohol production in America. This shared narrative among homebrewers (then and now) was repeated by Charlie Papazian in his 1984 manual *The Complete Joy of Homebrewing*, which explained their hobby's poor legal standing as the result of a stenographer's error in omitting the words "and/or beer" from the legislation that legalized home winemaking after Prohibition. Such an accidental ban would have surely been unjust, but the evidence in the legislative record reveals a less haphazard approach to lawmaking.[175]

Prohibition changed beer and all other forms of alcohol (except sacramental wines and a few other spiritual and medicinal exceptions) from taxable products into illicit potions. With this transition, the enforcement priority shifted from prosecuting tax evasion to preventing *all* manufacture of alcohol at home or otherwise (with greater or lesser degrees of zeal among the agents charged with this task). When repeal arrived, lawmakers looked back to earlier regulations as the basis for the new legal drinking regime. The Revenue Act of 1918 permitted licensed winemakers to enjoy two hundred gallons per year of their product tax free, and repeal legislation kept this clause.[176]

Homebrewing *beer* wasn't mentioned in the legislation before or after Prohibition—all of the language around beer was related to how to tax it upon removal from the brewery—but the legal framework around all manner of alcohol production shifted during Prohibition from absence implying legality to requiring an affirmative declaration of legality. Thus, an area that had been invisible to the law gradually became gray and eventually black-and-white. By the 1960s, homebrewers were seeking an enumerated legal sanction for their activities.

The hang-up with homebrew was that regulators were worried about wort, which is the sugar-rich liquid produced by steeping malted barley or other grains in hot water ("mashing," in brewer's parlance). With the skillful addition of hops and the proper brewer's yeast, the wort becomes beer, but wort can also be diverted into a distilling process to produce whiskey. Although brewers and distillers emphasize different flavor profiles in the mashing process, officials with the Bureau of Alcohol, Tobacco, and Firearms (ATF) were concerned that homebrew operations could be used as fronts for moonshining. As Congress debated homebrewing in 1978, the ATF dropped its opposition to legalization but maintained that homebrewers should be required to obtain a license from the U.S. Treasury Department and keep fewer than thirty gallons of homebrew on hand at any given moment. An attorney for the Treasury Department explained that "for enforcement and revenue protection purposes, registration is necessary in the case of homebrew since the process requires the production of a mash fit for distillation."[177]

In Congressional hearings, Senator Alan Cranston of California mocked the idea that "hordes of 'phantom moonshiners' are lurking the basements and closets of ordinary citizens who make beer in their homes," and he contended that the licensing requirement for home winemakers, which had been in place since Prohibition was repealed, was burdensome on the government and cost more to enforce than the license fees provided. Instead, Cranston proposed a bill that eliminated the registration requirement for winemakers and provided "equal treatment for homebrewers" with the other aspects of the home winemaking law. His amendment, popularly referred to as the "Homebrew Beer Equality Act" (HR 1337), was passed by Congress and signed into law by President Jimmy Carter, a well-known teetotaler during his presidency, in October 1978.[178]

Carter's signature legalized homebrewing at the federal level, but the Twenty-First Amendment repealing Prohibition was clear that states have the final say over alcohol production and sales within their borders. Therefore, each individual state would have to opt in before its citizens could lawfully enjoy their own brews. A small number of states—including Washington, Oregon, and Nebraska—had affirmed the right to homebrew in statutes adopted shortly after repeal, perhaps assuming that homebrewing wouldn't attract the interest of federal regulators any more than it had before Prohibition. A few more, including Hawaii and (by just a few months) California, helped force the reconsideration of homebrewing's legality by passing homebrew laws in the 1970s in spite of the by then well-known federal interpretation to the contrary. A larger group of states legalized homebrewing by default in the wake of the Cranston bill's passage, either through existing legislation that actively deferred to federal law in matters of alcohol regulation (such as in Montana and Arizona) or through a more passive interpretation of state laws that didn't explicitly ban homebrewing (as was the case in Nevada).[179]

Once the federal law was in place, the majority of remaining states followed suit one by one. Strangely, Colorado fell in the middle of the pack, only legalizing homebrew in 1986. There doesn't seem to be a good reason for the delay, leaving us to wonder if there wasn't a rush because legislators knew people were brewing at home anyway and couldn't be bothered to craft and vote on a new statute.[180]

A few states held out into more recent years, but when Alabama and then Mississippi finally dropped their resistance in 2013, homebrewing was at last legal in all fifty states. Thirty-five years after President Carter became the object of homebrewed toasts across the country, and during the administration of another well-known homebrewer-in-chief, President Barack Obama, legal homebrewing was the law of the land.

Although illegality was certainly a barrier for some (and perhaps part of the appeal for others), homebrewing's popularity was on the rise well before the stroke of Carter's pen in 1978. Rather than scarcity, the rise of homebrewing in the 1960s and '70s was driven by the lack of desirable options. Beer aficionados wanted better beer and sometimes spoke of the era's ubiquitous mass-produced light lagers as though they were the undrinkable spoiled swill that had plagued early colonists. In the absence of good commercial options, they figured that they had to brew it themselves. In stovetop brew kettles and improvised mash tuns, these brewers fermented a new era of American beer.

Today, homebrewing is legal across the nation, and the craft segment of the brewing industry is flourishing. Many observers trace this success back to the scofflaw fermentations of the small cadre of homebrewing advocates who openly pursued their passion for a better pint in the 1960s and '70s. These beer-loving zymurgists built on a long heritage of American homebrewing, but by successfully advocating for the legalization of their hobby, they catalyzed the growth of a dynamic new segment within the American brewing industry—one that took hold particularly strongly in Colorado, where people came to play outside and stayed for a few craft beers.

"RELAX. DON'T WORRY. HAVE A HOMEBREW."

Boulder, Colorado, in the mid-1970s was hardly a button-down kind of town. So it raised some eyebrows when a man in a shirt and tie registered for Charlie Papazian's homebrewing class.[181] "I was forewarned that a suspicious-looking character had registered for my class," Papazian recalled decades later. "And, sure enough, he showed up, in the mid-'70s, to my class wearing a white button-down shirt with black tie—the only guy in Boulder, probably, in a white shirt and a black tie!"

Papazian figured that the man was an agent with the Bureau of Alcohol, Tobacco, and Firearms (ATF), the agency charged with enforcing the federal prohibition against homebrewing. But Charlie went ahead with the class anyway: "I introduced the people in the class and gave them my normal spiel that [homebrewing is] illegal but don't sell it and you probably won't get hassled. He rolled up his sleeves and helped with a few batches of beer that we made. I think he came to two or three classes and then I never heard from him again."[182]

Whether the dapper man was indeed a fed or simply a curious attendee with a formal fashion sense, Papazian kept teaching the homebrewing course for a decade—on the wrong side of state and federal law all the while.

The easygoing atmosphere that left a well-dressed man sticking out in Boulder came in part from the city's growing counterculture ethos. In Boulder and in other "crunchy" granola-loving hippie hangouts across the country, a reaction against the mass-produced culture of the previous generation was taking hold. Homegrown vegetables were replacing canned

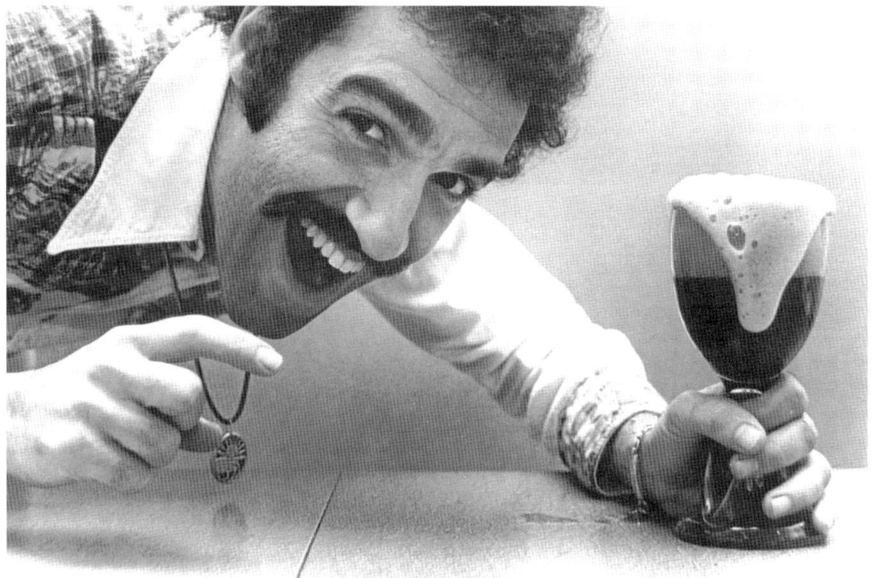

The guru of homebrew, Charlie Papazian might just be the most celebrated homebrewer since George Washington. *Courtesy of the Brewers Association.*

varieties, and some beer drinkers applied the same logic as they replaced corporately brewed canned suds with homebrew. Rejection of anything mass produced was all the rage in the mid-1970s, and lifestyle purveyors like the *Whole Earth Catalog* offered organic products from small-scale producers in an emerging do-it-yourself culture. Boulder's reputation as "Berkeley without the oxygen"—a high-altitude hippie hangout in the mythic Rocky Mountain West—acted like a magnet for socially conscious eco-friendly home-seekers, for many of whom homebrewing was an intriguing hobby. In that DIY atmosphere, homebrewing's appeal wasn't just that it could provide novel and more flavorful beers in a market dominated by industrially brewed American lager. It was an expression of a cultural shift toward valuing local things made in your own home or community.[183]

"[N]ow that growing your own (food, dope, hair, you name it) is hip," one widely reprinted underground newspaper article proclaimed in 1971, "it's time to resurrect the Dope of the Depression—Homebrew." The author extolled homebrewing as an "exercise of craft" that offered "good vibes from using something you make yourself, plus an improvement in quality" over the products sold by "Augustus [*sic*] Busch and the other fascist pigs who [were] ripping off the Common Man."[11] Not everyone making their own beer in the 1970s was quite so angry at big beer, but a strain of prevailing sentiment certainly held that Americans had become complacent and that their beers reflected the blandness of mass-produced American life and an ignorance of what else was out there.[184]

Papazian, if not quite as zealous about espousing this viewpoint, was something like its embodiment. Over hundreds of batches of homebrew, he explored a kaleidoscope of styles and flavors that most American beer drinkers had long forgotten. Homebrewing, once just a hobby, became his career. Fifty(ish) years after moving to Colorado, Charlie Papazian is known around the world as a brewing guru. A household name for any beer nerd worth their carboy, Charlie might just be the most celebrated American homebrewer since George Washington.

And for good reason. His long list of accomplishments contains notable highlights such as: cofounder of the American Homebrewing Association, creator of the Great American Beer Festival, author of an authoritative beer-styles guide used around the world, and cofounder of the Brewers Association, today's craft brewing industry trade group. His infectious love of good times and good beer brought about a homebrew revolution that, thanks to fortuitous timing and a cadre of friends and colleagues, launched Colorado's craft beer industry.

The homebrewing movement taking off in Boulder in the mid-1970s was part of an international awakening. American GIs returning from overseas postings and travelers taking advantage of newly affordable international flights helped push the movement forward, giving aspiring homebrewers the chance to taste beers that weren't available in the United States. British beer became particularly influential, partly because English brewing traditions focus on ales that are easier to make at home than lagers and partly because they simply brought more flavors to the glass than one-note mass-made American lagers. Stateside, homebrewing communities eager to make English styles for themselves coalesced around key figures such as Fred Eckhardt in Portland, Byron Burch and Jack McAullife in the San Francisco Bay area, Merlin Elhardt in suburban Los Angeles, and Charlie Papazian in Boulder.

Many of these homebrewers celebrated the new breweries that were starting to appear on the West Coast. Fritz Maytag, heir to the Maytag appliance fortune, had purchased San Francisco's failing Anchor Brewery in 1965 to preserve one of the nation's few remaining local breweries. He dedicated himself to learning brewcraft, embracing the historic local style called steam beer (which uses lager yeast to ferment at warm ale temperatures) with an artisan's dedication to quality and reviving the brewery's fortunes. It was an experiment in small-scale brewing, and it proved there was a market for something other than the big brewers' light lagers. As Maytag's enterprise was taking off, Jack McAuliffe, a navy veteran who had developed an affinity for the beers he had tasted in Scotland as a nuclear submarine mechanic, made a pilgrimage to Anchor. The visit inspired him to combine his mechanical talents and his passion for flavorful beer into a vocation. McAuliffe opened the New Albion Brewery in Sonoma, California, in 1976. It was the first new microbrewery to open in the United States since Prohibition and a signal moment for the brewing industry. Craft beer was here.[185]

It was no coincidence that homebrewing—and ultimately craft brewing—took hold along the West Coast and in the Rocky Mountains; these areas of the West were home to progressive hubs with wealthy residents and natural amenities that offered ample opportunity for recreation. These were the qualities putting cities at the forefront of economic and cultural shifts taking place across the country. But in western cities, the changes that spurred the homebrewing movement happened at a pace and with a totality that utterly reconfigured social, economic, and natural landscapes across the region. The transformation was so impactful that it begged historians to come up with a name to describe it. What they landed on was the "New West."[186]

The term "New West" is shorthand for a transition—a process, really, of western economies moving from a reliance on extractive industries to economies where amenity-based industries (think outdoor recreation and tourism) are increasingly significant. The scholars who throw this shorthand around aren't just focused on the dollars and cents. They've figured out that the New West is a different place socially and culturally too. As the economic landscape morphed, it inevitably reshaped the region's social fabric, shifting the demographics (and politics) of countless communities and entire states throughout the Intermountain West. But in few places has the New West's transformative impact been as pronounced as in Colorado, where the landscape's allure has fueled sustained population growth and economic development along the Front Range and throughout much of the High Country since the 1960s.

Like traditional industries such as hardrock mining, ranching, and energy development, the New West is rooted in the unique attributes of Colorado's landscape. But unlike the mineral and grazing bonanzas of earlier rushes, New Western economies are not aimed at extracting and selling Colorado's natural resources. Instead, they draw value from Colorado's natural amenities: the mountains, rivers, (red) rocks, and natural respites that attract home-seekers and tourists eager to get outside and into nature. And as it started to take shape in the late 1960s and early '70s, a growing group of New Westerners—many of them with high-paying jobs in burgeoning cities along the Front Range—increasingly paid top dollar for (first or second or third) homes in or near the mountains, plus the gear and lift tickets necessary to enjoy their time off in the mythic Rocky Mountain West.

Whether someone was seeking thrills or solitude, Colorado's high country was *the* place to find that "Rocky Mountain High" John Denver sang about—himself a New Westerner who'd come to Colorado to revel in the mountain lifestyle. His mountain music topped the charts in 1972 and '73, and those years of popularity for "Rocky Mountain High" corresponded to the state's largest population growth since the gold rush. As the decade progressed, former mining towns once mired in decline were morphing into glittering resorts. What had been small communities struggling to stave off economic collapse a few decades before—towns like Aspen, Breckenridge, Crested Butte, and Steamboat Springs—were suddenly transformed by the lure of federally designated public lands and carloads of tourist dollars.[187]

In just twenty years, Colorado grew from a place that Americans on either coast might have derided as a "flyover state" into one of the most desirable places in the country to live—and, not by coincidence, one of the best places in the country to grab a beer. For a particular but growing subset of these westerners—both new arrivals drawn by the region's amenities and born-and-bred residents who cherished the same things—enjoying more flavorful beer was an expression of the higher quality of life that was defining the New Western lifestyle. Sharing a homebrewed beer—with its subtle hints of authenticity, status, and appreciation for quality—was well suited to sitting around a campfire, taking in the vista from a mountain peak, or relaxing après-ski and reveling in the good fortune of calling such a place home. And for one New Westerner in particular, it was just this kind of lifestyle that made Colorado so alluring that he packed up his newly minted nuclear engineering degree and moved across the country.

Charlie Papazian was born in New Jersey and grew up walking rural roads in dairy country. It was an upbringing that established a lifelong love of time spent outdoors. While he was studying nuclear engineering and education at the University of Virginia in Charlottesville, a neighbor introduced him to homebrewing by way of a rough recipe involving a can of malt extract, some sugar, water, and a little bread yeast. The concoction tasted better to Papazian than anything he could buy commercially, and homebrew had the added advantage of being less expensive than premade stuff. He started reading up on homebrewing methods and was soon producing (then illegal) beer with his friends. After college, he headed west, finding his way to Boulder and the wealth of opportunity it offered for hiking, camping, and enjoying nature.[188]

Arriving in Boulder in 1972, Papazian soon found a job teaching at a local school. While educating children was his day job, he also taught adults the art of homebrewing in the classes he offered at Boulder's Community Free School. It was there that he met his friend and future brewing partner Charlie Matzen. Over the next several years, the Charlies developed a dedicated corps of fellow homebrewers and friends, and in December 1978, the pair cofounded the American Homebrewers Association (AHA). "We thought about it for an entire year because we realized it would be a pretty good commitment on our time to found an organization like that," Papazian recollected. "And then we decided to publish our first magazine."

As they pasted together page proofs with rubber cement, the pair were unaware of the legislative effort to legalize homebrewing being undertaken by Senator Alan Cranston at the same time. "We founded the American Homebrewers Association in complete ignorance that the law was going to be changed. We had no clue. It was something that we were not connected to," explained Papazian. But their timing couldn't have been better and couldn't have seemed more intentional. Papazian and Matzen published the inaugural issue of the homebrewing magazine *Zymurgy*—a newsletter whose name was a reference to the study of yeast fermentation—and founded AHA just months after President Carter signed off on legal homebrewing.[189]

The magazine and AHA grew quickly as homebrewers all over the United States (and Canada) came out of the legal shadows clamoring for recipes, tips, and tricks to improve the beers they were brewing. Initially stunned by the popularity of their publication, Matzen and Papazian quickly realized that their tiny, Boulder-based AHA was tapping into a deep vein of popular interest in homebrewing. *Zymurgy* spawned a network of people curious about making their own brews and amassed a body of knowledge that would ferment a national passion for great-tasting beer.[190]

Rejecting bland beers on offer from large breweries, *Zymurgy* contributor Alan Tobey announced in 1983 that the rise of home and small-scale brewers meant that the new brewers could leave behind the "thin and watery stuff in a carbonated can."[191]

Papazian and Matzen's knowledge of and enthusiasm for homebrewing was infectious. Over the next few years, the duo gathered a dedicated following of fellow homebrewers. Between formally organized homebrewing classes and informal parties, the Charlies were at the epicenter of an ever-

Above: Charlie Papazian's homebrew hobby turned into a career. He's been supporting and teaching aspiring homebrewers for more than fifty years. *Courtesy of Charlie Papazian.*

Right: Charlie Papazian pressurizes a keg at a Beer & Steer event in the late 1970s. *Courtesy of Charlie Papazian.*

growing homebrewing movement emanating from Boulder and drawing together like-minded brewers. While interest in homebrewing came from all across the nation, in the 1970s and early '80s the largest concentration of carboys was out west. It was where Papazian and his fellow brewers lived, not necessarily because it was where they had to be because of their jobs but because it was where they wanted to spend their time off.[192]

For Papazian and Matzen, some of these opportunities to play outside came in the form of huge "Beer & Steer" parties the duo threw near Boulder. The first was in 1975 on private land near Sugarloaf Mountain. By 1979, it had migrated to a site that became the Heil Valley Ranch open space. The party combined Matzen's love for good food, Papazian's brewing expertise, and the pair's shared love for convivial good times. It featured pit-roasted meat, local music, and lots and lots of homebrewed beer stored in a hand-built ice chest packed with snow lugged down from higher elevations. The one hundred or so attendees of the first Beer & Steer were mostly acquaintances of Papazian and Matzen or were Papazian's homebrewing students at the Community Free School. Despite a small mishap in which an overpowered spit turner lobbed hunks of raw beef at high speed, Beer & Steer was wildly successful and spawned a yearly tradition. In fact, in 1982 the third Beer & Steer drew more than four hundred participants from all over.[193]

For many early revelers already familiar with the burgeoning craft beer movement through their association with Papazian and Matzen, Beer & Steer parties were more than simply excuses to drink beer with friends in the woods outside of Boulder. Once word of the gatherings spread through the community, annual attendance turned into a marker of insider status. Recounting stories of partying inside the frigid cloud that engulfed Beer & Steer II or talking about the revelers who parachuted into Beer & Steer IV was a powerful means of self-identification that transformed an impromptu gathering of people with shared interests into an extremely popular social event. By the time of Beer & Steer IV, it was such a big deal that one of the organizers overheard a ticketless would-be reveler remark that he was "going to show up anyway," despite increasing attempts to control attendance.[194]

For Papazian and Matzen, collective enjoyment of beer paired naturally with outdoor recreation. Beer & Steer parties came to shape beer culture around the country as *Zymurgy* readers were treated to annual accounts of the hijinks. In this way, Colorado homebrewers not only grew used to enjoying their brews against a mountain backdrop but also began to associate beer drinking with the culture of outdoor recreation that was emerging on the Front Range. They learned what beer drinkers across Colorado know instinctively today: beer pairs well with playing outside.[195]

Since it was founded within sight of the striking sandstone Flatirons formations that serve so well as a mountain backdrop for Boulder, it's understandable that a certain appreciation of the great outdoors would permeate the culture at the growing American Homebrewers Association. It was certainly an attitude that seeped into their early publications. In the fall 1979 issue of *Zymurgy*, Papazian penned a column titled "Traveling with Homebrew." Full of tongue-in-cheek quips like, "If you plan to backpack, remember that alcohol is lighter than water," and "Homebrew is also terrific for repelling / forgetting centipedes, scorpions, rattlesnakes, cockroaches, ants, wind, rain, snow and flat tires," the article was focused on the kind of traveling done in the wilderness and on foot.[196]

Plus, Papazian's assertion that "it's not only EASY but practical to take homebrew along—even to remote areas," suggests that *Zymurgy* readers in the late '70s were becoming more familiar with outdoor recreation as a means of escaping demanding post-industrial confines like fluorescent-lit offices and gridlocked commutes. Dialing back his witticisms for just a moment, Papazian declared, "Most of us need some time for our nervous systems to leave the working world worries behind." The addition of homebrew to a backpacking trip would "keep your mind off of those worries until the moment you must return." Americans, particularly those out west, were increasingly taking to the outdoors to deal with the stress of modern life. With the introduction of the Wilderness Act of 1962, the federal government codified that there are some places with such natural splendor (a fair few in Colorado) that they should be left untouched—"untrammeled by man" in the parlance of Congress. Along with major advances in outdoor recreation equipment like the invention of nylon tents, lightweight waterproof clothing, and synthetic insulation later in the decade, it was easier, cheaper, and more comfortable to make prolonged trips into the woods. And thanks to Charlie, beer was coming along for the ride.[197]

The Beer & Steer parties cultivated a devoted community of homebrewing enthusiasts who sustained the annual celebration. But as the community grew into an industry in the 1980s and '90s, its innovative beermakers needed a more accessible, open, and just plain bigger event to keep pace with the thirst for the new generation of American beers they were brewing. Recognizing the evolving need, Charlie Papazian established the Great American Beer Festival in 1982 to do just that, and the GABF quickly supplanted Beer & Steer as the premier event in Colorado brewing.

Attendees enjoy the very first Great American Beer Festival, held in Boulder in 1982. *Courtesy of the Brewers Association.*

Following a 1982 visit to the Brewers Association of America's annual gathering, where he met brewers and executives from larger regional breweries, Papazian started to think about what it would take for homebrewers to turn pro. He was determined to expand the demand for craft brews and to start building connections among small-batch brewers. To this end, the AHA decided that its annual homebrewing competition should be aimed at a wider audience, and the Great American Beer Festival was born. Merging their fourth annual homebrewing competition with the GABF, Papazian and Matzen printed announcements in *Zymurgy* inviting guests from all over the country to come to Boulder on June 4, 1982. That first year, about 850 people took them up on the invitation.[198]

Budding professionals learned fast that the GABF offered a chance to rub elbows with other craft brewers and get help from the big breweries like Coors. The generally convivial atmosphere allowed craft beer pioneers to gather tips and pointers on beer making and beer marketing from larger, more experienced firms while gathering ideas for new styles from fellow homebrewers.

To bring some consistency to how they discussed the diverse and unfamiliar styles of beer being poured at that first festival, the program offered instructions on how to taste and talk about various styles of ale and lager.[199] By 1982, homebrewers and craft beer drinkers were accumulating experience with different kinds of ales and lagers, but they didn't have a common method of identifying or communicating about the tastes that defined the various styles. Characterizations of beers as light, bitter, or sweet almost fit the bill but were too broad and didn't convey the special qualities of a truly innovative beer or do much to differentiate between beers of similar styles. As such, the GABF's organizers drew on existing beer knowledge and on the established language of food and wine tasting to describe the various flavors that characterized each style of beer. Words like *flowery* were appropriated to describe the bitter, hoppy scent and flavor of pale ales, while *malty* was coined to convey the sweet, earthy flavor of darker brown ales, porters, and stouts. *Zymurgy*'s publication of tasting notes was an effort to expand the community of educated and appreciative beer lovers at a time when the craft brewing industry was struggling to get off the ground and every beer counted.

Over the next decade, the GABF would expand to include dozens more breweries, necessitating a move to more spacious accommodations in Denver. Its most important contribution to the rise of craft brewing was putting homebrewers in touch with beer industry professionals who often generously helped the upstarts work out the issues involved in scaling from small-batch home systems into commercial enterprises. Picking brains and making personal connections, homebrewers at the GABF learned how to make beer in large batches while maintaining quality and freshness.

Within the supportive networks of the American Homebrewers Association and the Great American Beer Festival, more local homebrewers honed their craft and felt confident in taking the next step: seeking out startup capital and making the leap from amateur to professional. Pioneering hobbyists were soon opening their own microbreweries all across the country, but Colorado was on the leading edge of the nascent craft beer movement thanks in no small part to the quality of life its natural amenities offered.

Breweries that are now household names across the state—Boulder Beer, Odell, Wynkoop, Ska, Great Divide, New Belgium, Avery, Oskar Blues and more—made the same uncertain bet on Colorado's future as Frederick Solomon and Adolph Coors had one hundred years before. Just like it did in the late 1800s, betting on beer paid off, one bottle (or can) at a time.

THE MICROBREW REVOLUTION

It all started back in the late '70s when Rudolph Ware and David Hummer were physics PhDs at the University of Colorado's Joint Institute for Laboratory Astrophysics. Using a hodgepodge of jury-rigged equipment, Ware and Hummer had been experimenting with the recipes they found in Charlie Papazian and Charlie Matzen's *Zymurgy* magazine along with their own homebrewed concoctions. As the story goes, after a faculty party featuring Ware's and Hummer's homebrew, a coworker asked the pair if there was anything left of the beer. When it turned out that the brew was gone, folks started asking when more would be available and whether they could buy it. And thus, in 1979, a brewery was born.

Initially housed in a goat shed outside of Hygiene, Colorado, Boulder Brewing Company would gain notoriety for winning one of the first gold medals in the porter beer category at the 1982 Great American Beer Festival. Ware, Hummer, and their third partner, Al Nelson, certainly weren't the first American homebrewers to make the leap into craft brewing, but they were the first to do so in Colorado—snapping up just the forty-third brewing license in the United States at the time. More importantly, they were the first "microbrewery" to take off outside of the West Coast. Drawing on ale brewing traditions undergoing their own revival across the pond thanks to British brewing pioneer Michael Jackson (think less moonwalk and more beer talk), Boulder Beer introduced many Coloradans to stouts, porters, pale ales, and barleywine—beers that came out of an English beer tradition. Ale, which had been largely erased from America's brewing industry and beer palate after Prohibition, was suddenly making a return to prominence. Dark, roasty, and handmade with care, Boulder Beer's porter was a special revelation to the small but growing cadre of microbrew enthusiasts.[200]

While California might have been the vanguard of small-batch beer, Boulder Beer was the first microbrewery to open in a non-coastal state, so the fact that the Denver Metro Area became home to leaders in craft brewing was due in part to the area's qualities as a hub of outdoor recreation and in part to the culture of expanding knowledge and appreciation—what some would call connoisseurism—that Papazian and the American Homebrewers Association helped to launch at the Great American Beer Festival.

Boulder Beer's ascent to notoriety and the rapid expansion of its brewing capacity paved the way forward for Colorado. Within the next two decades, an almost unbelievable proliferation of new breweries offered thirsty Coloradans a chance to identify with a local product and distinguish themselves as members of what was then an exclusive club. Boulder Brewing

These early ambassadors of homebrewing helped bring the hobby back to the United States. Here, they're sharing a brew at Boulder Beer in 1981. *Front row, from left*: British beer authority Michael Jackson, Boulder Beer brewmaster Otto Zavatone, and homebrew journalist Fred Eckhardt. *Second row, from left*: American Homebrewers Association founder Charlie Papazian, Boulder Beer cofounder Al Nelson, famed California homebrewer Al Andrews, and Tom Burns of Cartwright Brewing Company. *Back row, from left*: homebrewers Steve Gering and Lee Damkoehler. *Courtesy of the Brewers Association.*

Company's success was obviously the result of a variety of factors, but in this case, the forces of history that allowed for a successful brewing operation converged at a specific place and time in western history.[201]

But as appealing as beer bottled in a goat shed may have been to Colorado connoisseurs, some early festival attendees realized that professional-scale bottling and distributing were capital-intensive operations requiring lots of specialized knowledge. So some would-be bottlers shied away from packaging altogether after discovering that brewpubs could be another means of getting beer into consumers' hands and stomachs.

America's first brewpubs opened on the West Coast, and it wasn't long before Denver and the rest of the state caught on. Brewpubs were still illegal in Colorado in the early 1980s thanks to Prohibition and the convoluted laws it left behind. But small-batch beer's growing popularity across the state drew the attention of restaurateurs eager to cash in on the phenomenon taking off on the West Coast. Lobbyists did their jobs, and by the late 1980s the law was changed and the race was on to open Colorado's first brewpub.

Jim and Bill Carver—brothers who grew up working in Milwaukee bakeries—weren't strangers to hard work or the science of fermentation. Like so many others, the pair moved out to Colorado in the '80s to take advantage of the high-country lifestyle. Their Winter Park bakery kept itself afloat selling massive cinnamon rolls and scratch-made meals to tourists visiting the ever-expanding ski resort cut into the Arapaho National Forest just a few miles up US-40. But Winter Park sits in a high-mountain valley that gets frigidly cold in the winter. Together with the way their tourist-dependent business dried up in the summer months, the cold left the Carver brothers looking for easier weather and a more year-round economy. After selling their namesake bakery in 1987, they moved southward to a small college community tucked beneath the San Juan Mountains.

Durango was a different town back then. In the midst of a nationwide recession, the brothers recall boarded-up shops next door to their bakery in a town that had yet to experience the population influx and economic benefits of Colorado's outdoor recreation boom. Luckily for Durango, Carver Brothers Bakery was an instant hit. With its fresh bread baked daily and handmade preserves, the place was a must-stop breakfast and lunch haven for visitors and Durangans alike. Because they built their success on homemade products, when the brothers contemplated expanding into dinner service in 1988, they knew that having a handmade product on the menu would be essential. While homemade burger buns wouldn't be enough, small-batch beers might just fit the bill.

Buying some old brewing equipment from a burned-out Milwaukee brewery, the Carvers bakery crew started experimenting with new recipes. They had some expertise with bread yeast, but since buying brewer's yeast wasn't easy in Durango, the Carvers had to culture their own. With microbrew on the menu alongside common pub fare, Carvers cemented its status as a local hub as well as a critical stop for the ever-growing number of outdoor enthusiasts. Seasonal visitors from across the state and the region came through Durango on the way to hiking, skiing, fishing, or mountain biking in the storied San Juan Mountains, and a stop at Carvers was always on the menu. Even famed adventure writer Edward Abbey (an avowed beer drinker) stopped by Carvers in 1988. Although he'd never heard of small-batch beer, the brothers gave him some samples of their still-fermenting brew. Abbey, when asked what he thought of small-batch beer, replied by saying that it was a "damn-fine idea." Apparently he loved all of his samples.[202]

At the same time as the Carver brothers were helping revitalize downtown Durango, another group of entrepreneurs were looking to do the same for a long-neglected neighborhood in downtown Denver. Lower Downtown (or "LoDo") in the '80s wasn't a place that enticed many Denverites to hang out on a Friday or Saturday night. Decades of discriminatory real estate lending practices that divided Denver into racially restricted areas defined by red lines, coupled with the flight of white families out of the city center and near-in neighborhoods in the decades after World War II, had hollowed out the city. By the 1980s, most of Colorado's white middle class stuck to the suburbs, while opportunities for people living in Denver's urban core were severely limited.

John Hickenlooper recalls the effects of these policies, noting that in 1988 you could see tumbleweeds blowing down Wynkoop Street on a Friday evening. An unemployed geologist turned entrepreneur, Hickenlooper made a trip to a California brewpub while on a visit to Berkeley (the bay area was a leader in craft beer and brewpubs at the time), and he figured that Colorado's emerging microbrewed beer scene would help support a new restaurant in downtown Denver serving up its own beer. After scraping together as many dollars as they could, he and his partners Jerry Williams, Mark Schiffler, and Russel Schehrer opened the state's first brewpub. They beat the Carver Brewing Company in Durango by only about two months, thanks to a suddenly available rafting permit that allowed the Carver brothers a long-sought chance to boat the Grand Canyon before they turned their attention back to brewing.[203]

John Hickenlooper and partners Jerry Williams, Mark Schiffler, and Russell Schehrer opened Wynkoop Brewing in 1988 in the days before "LoDo" was part of every Denverite's vocabulary. *Courtesy of Wynkoop Brewing Company.*

According to Hickenlooper, Wynkoop Brewing Company's opening night was almost a fiasco, as hundreds of thirsty patrons rushed to the bar to buy pints for only twenty-five cents. The new brewery ran out of beer before eleven o'clock that night, selling more than six thousand plastic cups of fine English-inspired ales and leaving Hickenlooper wishing he'd charged double. Following on the heels of Wynkoop's and Carver's success, dozens of other brewpubs shaped growing Colorado towns in the next five years. Some familiar names include the likes of Boulder's Mountain Sun Pub & Brewery, Coopersmith's Pub & Brewing in Fort Collins, Phantom Canyon Brewing Company in Colorado Springs, and Breckenridge Brewery. But even among these quickly changing towns, the transformation of Denver's LoDo neighborhood was certainly the most dramatic.[204]

Wynkoop's opening came in the early days of a period that saw the reconfiguration of downtown Denver into one of the country's most desirable districts. New residents arrived by the tens of thousands each year, reversing the decades of stagnation and decline that had begun in the '60s and generating soaring rents and new challenges with gentrification. Wynkoop's ales, named for iconic places and industries of Colorado history, evoked a sense of place in a city that had yet to establish one for the new home-seekers pushing out longtime residents, many of them Black and Latino and whose families had lived in Denver for generations.

Wynkoop's success compounded growing investment from other entrepreneurs. The business surged through the early 1990s as wealthy investors capitalized on "Imagine a Great City" programs launched by Mayor Federico Peña and continued by the Wellington Webb administration that followed. Beer was already leading the way in LoDo, but its status as the drink of the times was confirmed with the arrival of the Colorado Rockies baseball franchise in 1993 and their new home at Coors Field, which opened in 1995 just a few blocks north of the Wynkoop and included an on-site brewery. As the ballpark was under construction, Great Divide opened a brewery, taproom, and bottling house in 1994 just a few blocks east. Other brewers joined the rush into the new millennium, opening taprooms throughout downtown alongside trendy restaurants and revitalized nightspots. In the span of just a few decades, longstanding demographic trends were turned on their heads as wealthy white residents reshaped Denver neighborhoods, often with local beer in hand.[205]

Beyond Denver, in a dynamic that recalled the late 1800s, craft breweries appeared in communities across the state wherever new arrivals were propelling rapid population growth—which seemed to be almost everywhere. By the late 1990s, Denver's new breweries were joining established operations like Odell's and New Belgium in Fort Collins; Boulder Brewing, Walnut Brewery, and Avery in Boulder; Phantom Canyon in Colorado Springs; Carver Brewing Company, Ska, Steamworks, and Durango Brewing in Durango; and Flying Dog in Aspen. Soon, mash tuns would be busy fermenting a craft boom in small towns turned recreation hotspots like Fruita and Buena Vista. Flavorful microbrews commanding the kind of prices that Coors used to get out east could be found in glass bottles in liquor stores across Colorado, while craft styles like India pale ale flowed from taps in nearly every corner of the state.[206]

Even Coors was getting in on the craft beer game, hiring brewmaster Keith Villa to create the company's Blue Moon Belgian white ale in its Sandlot Brewery tucked into the right-field side of Coors Field. All across Colorado, microbrewed local beer was a go-to drink for New Westerners who wanted to demonstrate their sophistication but who also just wanted something cold, relaxing, and delicious to enjoy after work or after playing outside. What was then known as "microbrewed" beer was a kind of liquid cachet that paired well with their vision of Colorado as the home of the good life. A knowledge of microbrewed beer and the palate to be able to appreciate it became, alongside carbon fiber mountain bikes and expensive ski gear, a marker of status and of the roots New Westerners were putting down in Colorado.[207]

In the early 2000s, buildings that housed working-class saloons in the nineteenth century rapidly transformed into upscale brewpubs. Even in boom-and-bust towns, the microbrew revolution brought about a dizzying turn of demographic and economic fortunes. Beer—a beverage steeped in working-class tradition—was now a symbol of refined appreciation of the good life among a growing class of New Westerners enjoying the economic benefits of the growth they were part of.

Beer and biking, brews and bootlaces—they were all indicators of a new culture emerging in the West, and one of Colorado's longest-lasting periods of economic growth.

CRAFTING THE CAN

Restaurateur Dale Katechis was struggling to make payroll. Like so many other New Westerners in the latter half of the twentieth century, Katechis came to Colorado to bike and brew near some of the Rockies' best trails. He opened Oskar Blues restaurant and brewery in 1997 in the small town of Lyons, where, like Carver Brewing Company in Durango, it became a staple for locals and tourists alike. In the summertime, Dale managed to sell enough barbecue and beer to keep the doors open and the lights on.

But when the snowflakes started to fly in nearby Rocky Mountain National Park, the tourists stopped coming. The winter months were lean at the restaurant, and on more than one occasion, Katechis was forced to use his pickup truck as collateral, selling it on a Friday and then buying it back on a Monday after the restaurant's earnings came in just so he could pay his staff.

Searching for a more stable all-season source of income, Katechis and his colleagues decided to try packaging their beer for sale beyond the restaurant. Tapping into Colorado's already competitive craft beer market in 2002 was going to be tough, but their decision to eschew the usual bottles and put Dale's Pale Ale in cans helped set their beer apart. By 2005, Oskar Blues was drawing national attention. In a *New York Times* taste test, Dale's Pale Ale won out over several other beers, in part because the can it came in preserved the beer's freshness. Writing about the novelty of drinking craft beer from a can, *Times* journalist Eric Asimov said, "Not long ago, cans represented all that was wrong with the assembly-line American beer industry. No craft brewer worth a copper brew kettle would even consider putting his precious ale in a can. But times have changed, and some brewers say that cans are lighter and easier to recycle than bottles, and offer complete protection against light." As Oskar Blues marketing director Chad Melis said of the article, "It was a well-respected third party with massive reach reinforcing everything we were saying. It fueled our fire to keep loading up the van and going to bike events, kayak events, music festivals, anywhere we could reach people one beer at a time."[208]

Today, canned beer is anything but a novelty. Mobile canneries make weekly rounds to even the smallest of taprooms. Thirty-two-ounce "crowlers"—a portmanteau of *can* and *growler*—mean that tap-fresh beer is available for patrons to take home from almost any brewery thanks to an affordable bartop can sealer invented at Oskar Blues. In short, breweries around the state are discovering what Bill Coors learned in 1959: aluminum cans are lighter, cheaper, and more recyclable than any other packaging material for beer. But what made the can *really* exciting for Colorado's consumers was the chance to finally toss one or two of their favorite flavor-packed pale ales in a backpack and enjoy it mid-mountain, an option the glass bottle's fragility and heft usually ruled out.

In the realm of items that come into and go out of fashion, the glass bottle is particularly pedestrian. Most of us stop thinking about the bottle we were just drinking out of the second it's empty. But to historians, archaeologists, and collectors, beer bottles are fantastically important. Beer, by its very nature, is a fleeting thing—it's a liquid that spoils rapidly without proper care. Even a beer delivered cold and fresh at the taproom—arguably the best way to drink a beer—should be enjoyed in a matter of minutes, not hours or years. But glass bottles are a whole different story. Unless they shatter, bottles will endure for centuries. Corrosion resistant and shockingly durable, glass bottles are some of the most common surviving relics from breweries that long ago shut off their kettles. In fact, beer bottles have been found in archaeological digs across Colorado, and a thriving collecting community of breweriana collectors pays top dollar for rare and well-preserved glass.

Craft brewers like Oskar Blues were heirs to this long history of packaging when they started looking into how they could get their beer onto liquor store shelves. But in the 1980s, the machinery to create cans was nowhere near as small as it is today. Canning lines were housed in huge warehouses and served by dedicated aluminum manufacturers who delivered millions of cans per year. So, for the guys in the goat shed from Boulder Beer and their fellow homebrewers gone pro, bottling wasn't just a good way to make craft beer stand out from the canned offerings of megabrewers. It was the only viable option.

Even as Colorado's craft beer scene blossomed in the late 1990s, Colorado craft brewers stuck with bottles. Glass—the stuff of fine wine and liquor for centuries—imparted an air of permanence and attention to quality. Despite advances in manufacturing that rendered cans inert, some consumers insisted that canned beer tasted like the metal it came in. Still others believed that bottlers cared more about their craft, in contrast to the canned stuff that journalist Mike Royko said "tasted like the secret brewing process involved running it through a horse." So when he started packaging his beer, Dale Katechis was well aware that aluminum cans carried a lowbrow stigma associated with mass-produced lagers. Conventional wisdom held that the social cachet of craft beer could not be sipped from cans. To the craft- or homebrew-consuming public, Coors and its canned counterparts represented a mainstream, corporate beer-brewing apparatus that had little appreciation for flavor or the evolving values of the New West.[209]

For these reasons, in the early years of the new millennium, convincing craft beer consumers to drink out of cans was a hard row to hoe. So Oskar Blues set out to buy bottling equipment. But before it committed itself, the brewery received what Chad Melis calls a "spam fax" from a company offering a one-at-a-time canning line.

"At first," Melis says, "like everybody else we laughed, it was pretty much a joke at that time." But a twinge of curiosity kept gnawing at the brewing team, and with Ball corporation's can manufacturing plant just down the road, Katechis and his coworkers decided to go see whether cans were a viable packaging option for a small brewery.

As things turned out, Ball was willing to manufacture cans for Dale's Pale Ale in small enough batches to make economic and logistical sense. When the minds behind Oskar Blues realized that cans are better for the brewery's bottom line while being better for the beer and better for the environment, the decision to put his beer in cans was what Melis calls "kind of a no-brainer."[210]

The can was an obvious point of departure from the ubiquitous bottle, and it eventually helped set the brewery apart by giving it a reputation for commitment to quality and supporting local businesses. But in 2002, with the stigma against canned beer firmly entrenched among craft beer drinkers, the Lyons-based brewery's employees figured that they needed to hit the road. Long days and nights of travel took Dale's Pale Ale and its blue can, emblazoned with an idyllic mountain backdrop, anywhere beer connoisseurs congregated. Most often, this entailed loading up the van and heading out to mountain bike races, kayaking exhibitions, and other outdoor events to show people that cans made it possible to play outside while enjoying great beer.

As word about their canned craft beer got around, the folks at Oskar Blues saw that cans and the outdoor-oriented culture they promoted were appealing strongly to the same growing market of New Westerners that was buying Boulder Beer's Singletrack Copper Ale or New Belgium's Fat Tire Ale. Chad Melis says that consumers told the Oskar Blues team how appreciative they were to finally have a craft beer they could take with them when they went skiing, hiking, or camping. Despite Charlie Papazian's valiant efforts in that 1979 *Zymurgy* article to convince beerlovers that they could take their favorite craft brew traveling with them through Colorado's spectacular landscapes, two decades of lugging heavy, clinking backpacks and mourning tragically shattered bottles had left recreationists longing for their favorite beer in cans. This new mobility, along with the can's eco-friendly recyclability, gave Oskar Blues a competitive advantage with New Westerners whose purchasing habits reflected a commodification of outdoor recreation and a desire for products that minimized environmental impact.

For these New Westerners, who are often amenable to spending good coin on top-flight equipment for their outdoor exploits, consuming craft beer while playing outside dovetailed with purchases of material markers of economic status on offer from Colorado outfitters like Melanzana and Moots cycles or larger brands like Patagonia and REI. And the aluminum can's infinite recyclability meant consumers were reducing their ecological impact by directing their dollars away from resource-intensive glass. Thus,

Dale's Pale Ale in its original cans. It was the first modern craft beer to be distributed in aluminum cans. *History Colorado, 2019.26.1.*

Oskar Blues was able to make craft beer in cans into a prominent icon of the amenity-driven economy of the twenty-first-century West.

As Melis put it, "We wanted to have a can—a clearly identifiable can—on everything. Whether you see an Oskar Blues tap handle, an Oskar Blues poster, or on the shelf at the liquor store, you see a lot of consistency in the cans. For us, that can was a symbol of a couple of different things: of quality craft beer; of environmentalism; and that active lifestyle that brought us all together in Lyons."[211]

Beer marketing continues to play on this synergy of environmentalism and active outdoor lifestyles despite the fact that neither outdoor recreation nor beer brewing are particularly environmentally friendly industries; even the most conscientious craft breweries have about a ten-to-one ratio of water used to beer brewed. Nevertheless, the nature motif on Oskar Blues cans is part of a culture of using a mountain scene to promote sales that started in the 1880s, and for years the brewery sponsored professional mountain bikers as well as Lyons's own community-oriented outdoor festival. Cheekily called Burning Can, the event was an integral part of the Lyons Outdoor Games and became a central feature of the town's weekend-long celebration of extreme sports and suds.

That festival and other outdoor recreation events like it weren't just a good way to get beer to consumers—they were an expression of an eco-conscious, amenity-driven consumer culture that's grown up around gear and beer in the American West.[212]

LESSONS FROM THE CRAFTSPLOSION

With roots stretching back arguably to the 1870s, Colorado's craft beer boom seems like it was a long time coming. But in reality, the explosion of craft brewing was a fairly recent phenomenon driven by the taproom boom.

Brewpubs were popular, but, increasingly, what became known as the "taproom"—where visitors can try a variety of beers either from one brewery or many on tap—is rising to prominence. Taprooms like the Copper Club in Fruita started opening around the state in the early 2000s, and tourism is supporting breweries far afield from the Front Range. Even in the wake of the COVID-19 pandemic, new breweries are still opening in mountain towns across the state. Even the tiny community of Fraser, population 1,400 in 2022, has three thriving craft breweries. And Ouray, nestled into its box canyon beneath the peaks of the San Juans, boasts a pair of breweries for its 900(ish) residents.

For many of these small mountain brewers, their popularity and their marketing are both explicitly tied to the idea that these are places for visitors and locals alike to gather with good friends after hiking a fourteener, swishing down the slopes, riding the rapids, or slaying some singletrack. They're anchors of the New Western lifestyle in communities that, a generation or two earlier, were on the wrong side of the state's boom-and-bust economic cycles.

All across Colorado, New Western dollars have been a lifeline. Communities long neglected have seen trendy taprooms boom. But the

After Oskar Blues founder Dale Katechis's bicycle was stolen, employees at the brewery built him a new one from scratch. Out of this gesture, REEB Cycles (*beer* spelled backward) was born. It still builds bikes in the century-old barn in Lyons that had housed the original canning line for Oskar Blues. *Courtesy of Oskar Blues Brewing Company.*

negative side effects that come with an influx of tourists and urban amenity seekers haven't been borne equally. Gentrification and out-of-reach housing are problems both city and mountain communities are desperate to solve.

In modern Colorado, craft breweries are simultaneously centers of growing community identity and drivers of inequity. And brewing as an industry is still striving to address its exclusion problem, despite years of efforts to be more accessible to brewers and beer-lovers of color. Latino-owned breweries like Raices and Black-owned breweries like Spangalang or Novel Strand in Denver represent welcoming community hubs in an industry that's slowly grappling with its legacy of exclusion. Raices owner Jose Beteta, a champion of getting the word out about Latino beer culture, founded Suave Fest—an unfortunately short-lived festival featuring Latino brewers—in Denver in 2019.

And after almost a century and half of systemic barriers to women brewers, the Colorado beer industry is coming around full circle. Woman-owned breweries like Holidaily, helmed by Karen Hertz in Golden, and Lady Justice, founded by a group of women in Aurora, are forging a new path for female brewers. And in another encouraging turn of the wheel of history, lager-style beers no longer just represent the ways women were pushed out of the brewing industry (nor, in Colorado's case, how they were excluded from the very beginning). Today, Ashleigh Carter of Bierstadt Lagerhaus in Denver has become one of the most celebrated lager makers in the country. She stands at the head of a rising number of women brewers, bringing the industry back to its historic roots as women reclaim their role as masters of the brew kettle.

As the state's brewing industry embraces these advances and keeps working toward crafting a community for all Coloradans, beer and outdoor recreation remain world-renowned hallmarks of the Colorado lifestyle. And the story of the state's brewing industry reflects the change and growth embodied in the phenomenon of the New West.

With more than four hundred breweries operating at the beginning of 2023, and more opening all the time, the craft beer sector contributes more to Colorado's economy per capita than it does in any other state, according to the Brewers Association. Denver hosted the fortieth anniversary of the Great American Beer Festival in October of 2022, and Golden is still home to (though no longer the headquarters of) the Coors brewery—the largest single-site brewery in North America. Thanks in part to Charlie Papazian and the craft beer revolution he started with his homebrew crew, it's the rare ski area café or mountain restaurant that has no local ale on offer, and brewery meetups are an integral part of local culture for communities all across the state. Homebrewing—an activity that started as a fringe hobby and a response to a lack of beer options among a select segment of comfortably wealthy and white New Westerners—now includes increasingly diverse communities of brewers and drinkers.

From La Junta to Grand Junction and from Fort Collins to Trinidad, beer is more than a quirky local commodity or a pleasant way to pass an afternoon. It's an integral part of people's Colorado lifestyles.

The story of how Colorado became one of the best places in the world to grab a pint is more than just a tale of ale. It's also an index for how Colorado has changed in the last half century. It's an amber (or pale yellow or malty black) lens through which we can better understand how today's Colorado came to be.

LAST CALL

We said this at the outset, and as we come to a close, it bears reiterating: Brewers are making good beer across these United States.

But the role beer has occupied in Colorado's story makes it an ideal elixir for illuminating larger trends that have shaped the place we're lucky to call home today. Colorado is a place where saloons once doubled as halls of government. A place that helped lead the nation into Prohibition and later helped lead the nation's craft beer renaissance. A place that remains home to the largest single brewery in the world and where beer can be an ambassador of the Rocky Mountain mystique and a flashpoint in the struggle for civil rights. In many ways, it's the beating heart of the industry today, where professional organizations like the Brewers Association and the American Homebrewers Association support brewers nationwide and where brewers and beer lovers gather every year by the tens of thousands for the Great American Beer Festival. Colorado is a place that requires a years-long commitment from any imbiber ambitious enough to raise a glass at every brewery in the state—a journey supported by more than sixteen thousand people who work in a brewing industry that generates more than $2.5 billion in economic impact annually.[213]

The historic currents that crafted Colorado have always had a measure of beer flowing through them, and today they continue to reveal a shifting landscape. As we conclude this book, Colorado's beer industry is once again poised to illuminate larger economic and social forces shaping our lives.

In what future historians will likely point to as an indicator of important trends we're still too close to see, in the span of one month—November 2019—Coloradans found out that *two* of the state's most iconic breweries were diluting their Colorado connections. In a move presaged by nearly two decades of mergers and acquisitions that diminished Coors' Colorado ties, the iconic Golden brewery announced that it was moving its headquarters from Denver to Chicago (although the production line is still in Golden). And just a few weeks later, New Belgium Brewing Company announced its sale to the Tokyo-based beverage company Kirin Holdings.

To the beer lovers of Colorado, among whose ranks the authors proudly count themselves, these moves might not be surprising. Especially because they followed earlier buyouts like Avery's sale of a majority stake in the company to a Spanish firm between 2017 and 2019 and Breckenridge's sale to the Belgium-based AB InBev in 2015. But they're noteworthy nonetheless. After nearly thirty years of expansion, the beer market has undergone a contraction in the face of stiff competition from distilled spirits, trendy hard seltzers, and (depending on whom you ask) marijuana. The moves echo the buy-ups, mergers, and foreign acquisition that swept through Colorado's brewing industry at the turn of the last century, proving once again that while history doesn't repeat, sometimes it rhymes.

In what can sound like another echo of the past, a growing interest in the harmful effects of alcohol on individual and public health seems to be gaining traction. Alcohol addiction and the myriad health effects overconsumption can cause the human body are ever-present concerns, and new warnings in popular media outlets about the risks of drinking are prompting some consumers to consume less or experiment with periodic personal prohibitions like "dry January," all of which has today's brewers bringing back the nonalcoholic beers brewers made at the outset of Prohibition.[214]

Concerns about economic consolidation and public health aren't new to the story of beer in Colorado. But today they're happening in a state that's markedly different from the place where the industry first took root.

The rise of the New West—with the premium it places on enjoying natural amenities over extracting natural resources—has transformed Colorado at a pace and a scale unrivaled since the gold rush. Colorado's economy no longer hinges on what can be grown in the field, felled in the forest, or dug out of the ground. More and more, the big money is flowing into the amenity economies of Colorado's resorts. In fact, one of the few ways modern Colorado towns resemble those ramshackle days of early settlement is in their plethora of spots for local suds.

Who will pour those suds and where those tap tenders might be able to live are open questions, at least right now. The most desirable outdoor lifestyle outposts (a list of communities that seems to grow longer every year) are bursting at the seams as longtime residents struggle to afford their own hometowns in the face of influxes of newcomers and the rising rents they bring along. Local cultures erode and communities fracture as workers are increasingly forced to commute from distant mountain valleys where the cost of living is more affordable to low-paying service industry jobs in the high-country heart of the New West. Meanwhile, many second homes sit empty for most of the year, economic imbalances grow more pronounced, and desirable communities throughout Colorado and the broader region are confronting the question of whether New Western economies will be able to sustain themselves, not to mention concerns over what's happening to the ecology of places straining to cope with so many new campers, hikers, snowmobilers, and bikers (to name but a few popular pastimes).

New Westerners are also starting to confront their history of racial and gender exclusion. Hardened racial barriers like red lines and discriminatory legislation, such as the GI Bill, imposed insulting and unjust limits on people of color and their ability to access the social and economic benefits of New Western economies. Prejudices against women in the beer industry still linger, although a new generation of influential female brewers continues to bust glass ceilings. The legacies of these policies and prejudices are evident in a glance across the taproom at nearly any brewery in Colorado and especially in the lift lines and checkout counters at outdoor outfitters who've long directed their marketing toward wealthy white home-seekers. Efforts at inclusion and diversification are starting to have an effect, but the question lingers: can a mature New West be a more inclusive place?

As the newness of the New West fades after almost seventy years of booming growth, it begs the question of what the region *is*, and what it will be, now that the novelty is wearing off. Historical studies like this one can help illuminate the contours of the New West and how we got to now, but they don't really reveal where the path into the future will lead. Future historians will record the next cycles of social and economic change to remake the Rockies. The ones living (and writing) now can only point out what they see around them and hope to explain a bit of how this version of Colorado came to be.

Whatever comes next, though, beer is likely to stay in the story. Today's taprooms and neighborhood breweries bear only the slightest resemblance to

Colorado's early saloons. But zoom out past the family-friendly atmosphere many breweries cultivate, past the modern equipment, food trucks, and trivia nights, and what remains is a community gathering spot that plays a vital role in creating and sustaining the economic and social ties of diverse communities across the state. With more breweries than most of us can ever hope to visit, good beer flows in every corner of Colorado. And as it has for more than 150 years, beer still brings us together.

NOTES

First Round

1. Portions of the text in this chapter first appeared in Jason L. Hanson, "'Innocent of Hops': The Case of Colorado's First Craft Beer," October 14, 2014, CPR.org, and Jason L. Hanson, "Brewers Want the Best: Growing a Brewing Industry in the Centennial State," *Colorado Heritage* (September/October 2015): 16–23. Used with permission of Colorado Public Radio and History Colorado.
2. David Lavender, *Bent's Fort* (University of Nebraska Press, 1954), 52; Harold H. Dunham, "Ceran St. Vrain," in *Mountain Men and Fur Traders of the Far West*, ed. LeRoy Hafen (University of Nebraska Press, 1982), 146–65; J. Thomas Scharf, *History of St. Louis City and County*, vol. 2 (Louis H. Everts and Company, 1883), 1,330; James Neal Primm, *Lion of the Valley: St. Louis, Missouri, 1764–1980* (Missouri Historical Society, 1998), 194.
3. Bent's Fort was by no means dry. Guests could get wine or whiskey, which traveled well on the trail, or an ice-cold glass of lemonade year-round thanks to the storage of ice cut from the frozen Arkansas River. But those thirsting for a frosty brew were out of luck. Interview with Dr. Holly Norton, Colorado State Archaeologist, October 30, 2018.
4. Sam'l P. Arnold, *Eating Up the Santa Fe Trail* (University Press of Colorado, 1990), 67–68. Arnold offers a recipe for spruce beer that was common around western military bases, although it relies on a small amount of hops.
5. Theodore Borek, Curtis Mowry, and Glenna Dean, "Analysis of Modern and Ancient Artifacts for the Presence of Corn Beer: Dynamic Headspace Testing of Pottery Shards from Mexico and New Mexico," *MRS Proceedings* (2007): 1,047; "Did Early Southwestern Indians Ferment Corn and Make Beer?" Sandia press release, December 3, 2007; Patrick J. Abbot, "American Indian and Alaska Native Aboriginal Use of Alcohol in the United States," *American Indian and Alaska Native Mental Health Research* 7, no. 2 (1996).

6. See *Rocky Mountain News Weekly*, August 13, 1859, 2, for an early advertisement for J.B. Doyle & Company; Henrietta E. Bromwell, "Colorado Argonauts of 1858–1859," vol. 2 (typescript, 1926), 277; Jerome C. Smiley, *History of Denver: With Outlines of the Earlier History of the Rocky Mountain Country* (Times-Sun Publishing Company, 1901), 296, 301–2; Allen DuPont Breck, *The Centennial History of the Jews of Colorado* (Hirschfeld Press, 1960), 11–12.
7. Available biographies of John Good, several of which use largely the same language, commonly repeat these details. See William Columbus Ferril, ed., *Sketches of Colorado*, vol. 1 (Western Press Bureau Company, 1911), 237.
8. For a sense of the colorful and sometimes unsettling nature of everyday life during Denver's first year, see Libeus Barney, *Early-Day Letters from Auraria (Now Denver), Written to the Bennington Banner, Bennington, Vermont, 1859–1860* (A.J. Luddit Press, n.d.), History Colorado Collection, 978.883 B265e.
9. This story is repeated in Margaret Coel, Jane Barker, and Karen Gilleland, *The Tivoli: Bavaria in the Rockies* (Colorado and West, 1985), 6.
10. The conjecture that Good freighted the hops on his second trip is pure guesswork based on the fact that the first batch of beer wasn't brewed until the fall, and presumably the entrepreneurs would have brewed earlier if they could have. See *Rocky Mountain News Weekly*, November 24, 1859, 2, for mention of the first beer available to taste.
11. Solomon made the 1,700-mile round trip to St. Louis in twenty-six days during the fall of 1860, according to the *Rocky Mountain News*, September 21, 1860, 3. However, there's no record of him making such a journey in 1859.
12. Maxine Benson, "Tivoli: Yesterday and Today," typescript, Colorado Historical Society, 1970, 4.
13. "The Rialto Mine," *Denver Times*, July 9, 1899, 13; Bromwell, "Colorado Argonauts," 319.
14. *Rocky Mountain News Weekly*, November 24, 1859, 2; *Rocky Mountain News*, December 8, 1859, 3; *Rocky Mountain News*, December 14, 1859, 3.
15. *Rocky Mountain News Weekly*, July 12, 1872, 2.
16. Hanson, "Innocent of Hops"; *Rocky Mountain News Weekly*, January 11, 1860, 3; *Rocky Mountain News Weekly*, May 16, 1860, 5; *Rocky Mountain News*, April 19, 1861, 2; *Rocky Mountain News*, January 24, 1861, 3; *Rocky Mountain News*, June 21, 1862, 2; Benson, "Tivoli," 4–7; Coel, Barker, and Gilleland, *Tivoli*, 7–9.
17. Thomas J. Noel, *The City and the Saloon: Denver 1858–1916* (University Press of Colorado, 1996), 6, 12; Elliott West, *The Saloon on the Rocky Mountain Mining Frontier* (University of Nebraska Press, 1979), 27–30.
18. Noel, *City and the Saloon*, 6; West, *Saloon on the Rocky Mountain Mining Frontier*, 34.
19. West, *Saloon on the Rocky Mountain Mining Frontier*, 28.
20. Charles M. Clark, *A Trip to Pikes Peak and Notes Along the Way* (S.P. Rounds, 1861), 95.
21. Noel, *City and the Saloon*, 11–21, 121; West, *Saloon on the Rocky Mountain Mining Frontier*, 74–76.
22. West, *Saloon on the Rocky Mountain Mining Frontier*, 36–42.

23. Noel, *City and the Saloon*, 53–66; West, *Saloon on the Rocky Mountain Mining Frontier*, 42–43; Jon M. Kingsdale, "The 'Poor Man's Club': Social Functions of the Urban Working-Class Saloon," *American Quarterly* 25, no. 4 (October 1973): 472–89.
24. Royal Melendy, "The Saloon in Chicago," *American Journal of Sociology* 6 (November 1900): 289–306.
25. Noel, *City and the Saloon*, 14, 33–40, 53–66, 85–86.
26. West, *Saloon on the Rocky Mountain Mining Frontier*, 59–60.
27. West, *Saloon on the Rocky Mountain Mining Frontier*, 45–47; Robert Taft, "The Pictorial Record of the Old West: Custer's Last Stand—John Mulvany, Cassily Adams, and Otto Becker," in Paul Andrew Hutton, ed., *The Custer Reader* (University of Oklahoma Press, 2004), 424–62.
28. William Elliott West, "Dry Crusade: The Prohibition Movement in Colorado, 1858–1933," PhD diss., University of Colorado Boulder, 1971, 25–27; "Beer," *Rocky Mountain News Weekly*, July 30, 1873, 3; Harold T. Burns, "Cocktails Fit for Mornings Only, Says Old-Time Brewer in Denver," *Rocky Mountain News*, March 4, 1936. Burns quotes Frederick Neef.
29. Elliott West, "Beer: A Western—and Human—Tradition," *Journal of the West* 55, no. 2 (Spring 2016): 16; Noel, *City and the Saloon*, 81; West, "Dry Crusade," 28–29; William Kostka Sr., *The Pre-Prohibition History of Adolph Coors Company, 1873–1933* (Adolph Coors Company, 1973), 17.
30. West, "Dry Crusade," 25–27. The exact numbers are 22,902 barrels in 1878 and 234,735 in 1893.
31. Maureen Ogle, *Ambitious Brew: The Story of American Beer* (Mariner Books: 2007), 15.
32. Clyde L. King, *The History of the Government of Denver with Special Reference, to Its Relations with Public Service Organizations* (Fisher Book Company, 1911), 45, 100, 225; West, "Dry Crusade," 30–31.
33. Gunther Barth, *Instant Cities: Urbanization and the Rise of San Francisco and Denver* (Oxford University Press, 1975); Duane A. Smith, *Rocky Mountain Mining Camps: The Urban Frontier, 1860–1901* (University Press of Colorado, 1967); Duane Allan Smith, "Mining Camps: Myth vs. Reality," *Colorado Magazine* 44, no. 2 (1967): 93–110.
34. "Beer," *Rocky Mountain News Weekly*, July 30, 1873, 3; Noel, *City and the Saloon*, 12; "Beer Is 10 Cents a Glass at Billy Lindenmeir's," *Rocky Mountain News*, June 27, 1867, 4; "The Atlantic Garden," *Rocky Mountain News*, June 20, 1866, 1. By 1873, the four breweries operating in Denver were reputed to be manufacturing 2,500 barrels of lager beer (in addition to ale) every month, amounting to approximately 77,500 gallons (at 31 gallons per barrel) packaged in roughly 10,000 kegs. About half was consumed in and around the city and the other half shipped "outside of the territory," as far west as Salt Lake City.
35. *Rocky Mountain News*, October 22, 1860, 2, c3; Bayard Taylor in *Colorado: A Summer Trip* (GP Putnam and Son, 1867), 56. Taylor wrote, "Commencing at Black Hawk—where the sole pleasant object is the Presbyterian Church, white, tasteful, and charmingly placed on the last steps of Bates Hill, above the uniting ravines—we mount Gregory Gulch by a rough, winding, dusty road, lined with crowded wooden buildings: hotels, with pompous names and limited

accommodations; drinking saloons—'lager beer' being a frequent sign; bakeries, log and frame dwelling houses, idle mills, piles of rusty and useless machinery piled by the wayside.... [T]he houses, mills, drinking saloons, and shops continue just the same, and in another half-mile you find yourself in Central City."

36. *Rocky Mountain News*, February 24, 1865, 3; *Daily Mining Journal*, November 29, 1864, 3. The *Daily Mining Journal* of Black Hawk reported just three months earlier that beer was going for $7 per keg. To give a sense of the quantity required, a decade after this episode in 1874, the relatively small Schueler and Coors Brewery in Golden, founded only the year before, purchased 200,000 pounds of barley at a cost of $10,000 to produce more than 2,000 barrels of beer. As Coors was just getting started, the much larger Denver Brewing Company reported that it required 2.5 million pounds of barley a year and had paid out between $80,000 and $90,000 in 1874 to import barley from growers in Utah and California in addition to what it bought from local growers. *Rocky Mountain News*, February 7, 1875, 2; *Rocky Mountain News*, April 28, 1874, 4; *Rocky Mountain News*, January 16, 1875, 4.

37. "A Big Institution," *Aspen Daily Times*, April 24, 1892, 6; advertisement for "The Ph. Zang Brewing Co., Proprietors of the Rocky Mountain Brewing Company," May 8, 1892, 3; WestEgg.com Inflation Calculator. This "Big Institution" article appeared in multiple papers around the same time and may have been a form of "paid advertising" by the brewery, giving it a platform to respond to criticisms about its recent purchase by a British concern as well as reports of its strong-arm tactics with saloonkeepers (see Noel, *City and the Saloon*, 80) by emphasizing its contribution to the local economy. While perhaps unsavory, this type of article has the advantage of implying a certain reliability of the numbers quoted (perhaps with some exaggeration), since they came from the source. The notice for Zang's appeared regularly in the *Aspen Daily Times* in the early 1890s, boasting that Zang's had a capacity of "150,000 barrels per annum."

38. "Barley and Brewing," *Rocky Mountain News*, April 28, 1874, 4, c1; "Big Institution," 6; "Pells Buys Seed Barley," *Boulder Daily Camera*, February 13, 1907; *Colorado Transcript* (Golden), April 13, 1898. Even when they didn't supply the seed, brewers tried to incentivize growers to plant barley. In 1902, the Durango Beer and Ice Company offered bonuses for the largest barley growers in the area and guaranteed to buy all brewers barley up to 100,000 bushels grown in La Plata, Montezuma, and Dolores Counties (plus San Juan County, New Mexico) at a minimum price of $1.15 per 100 pounds. See the *Durango Democrat*, March 20, 1902, 4. The advertisement ran regularly in the paper for much of the spring.

39. "Pells Buys Seed Barley." Special thanks to Mona Lambrecht and the Boulder History Museum, which featured this article in the 2013 exhibit "Beer!: Boulder's History on Tap" (Boulder History Museum, March 1–October 27, 2013), for calling this to our attention.

40. *Rocky Mountain News*, January 14, 1875, 2.

41. "Beer," *Rocky Mountain News Weekly*, July 30, 1873, 3.

42. *Rocky Mountain News*, January 14, 1875, 2.

43. "Beer," *Rocky Mountain News Weekly*, July 30, 1873, 3.

44. Coel, Barker, and Gilleland, *Tivoli*, 6–7.

45. "Big Institution," 6.
46. *Denver Daily Times*, August 26, 1875, 4.
47. *Silver Cliff Rustler*, September 12, 1889, 2. On the same day, in an inauspicious juxtaposition for the hops grower, the paper also reported, "The Woman's Christian Temperance Union of Denver have expended nearly $4,000 the past year in their various benevolent enterprises," that the *Agitator* was a Prohibition paper just started in Pueblo, and that "The Florence brewery was burned to the ground last week. Loss about $20,000."
48. "Hop Growing Is Profitable: Farmers in State of Washington Making Big Money from Their Hop Fields—Why Not Start Industry Here?," *Fort Collins Weekly Courier*, September 29, 1911, 2.
49. *Rocky Mountain News*, January 11, 1874, 4. In 1874, the *Rocky Mountain News* noted a visit from C.C. Green, a principal in the firm Chas Green, Sons & Company of Hubbardsville, New York, who was "the principal correspondent of the Colorado brewers." Central and northern New York State was the premier hops-growing region in the United States in the nineteenth century. For a history of hop growing in New York, particularly Franklin County, see Thomas A. Rumney, "A Search for Economical Alternatives: Hops in Franklin County, New York During the Nineteenth Century," *Middle States Geographer* 31 (1998): 23–34.
50. Advertisement for "The Ph. Zang Brewing Co., Proprietors of the Rocky Mountain Brewing Company," May 8, 1892, 3; ad for the Palace Bar, *Creede Candle*, December 8, 1906, 4. Both ads appeared regularly.
51. *Fort Morgan Times*, February 22, 1889, 3.
52. For more on pre-contact cacao brewing in the Americas, see Arturo Gómez-Pompa, José Salvador Flores, and Mario Aliphat Fernández, "The Sacred Cacao Groves of the Maya," *Latin American Antiquity* 1, no. 3 (1990): 247–57, doi.org/10.2307/972163.
53. See Judith M. Bennett, *Ale, Beer, and Brewsters in England: Women's Work in a Changing World, 1300–1600* (Oxford University Press, 1996); Allison Schell, "Women + Beer, A Forgotten Pairing," National Women's Museum, 2016.
54. Schell, "Women + Beer."
55. Dave Thomas, *Of Mines and Beer!: 150 Years of Brewing History in Gilpin County, Colorado, and Beyond* (CreateSpace Independent Publishing Platform, 2012), 40.
56. "'Bass' Ale, the Standard Appetizer, Kept on Draughht [*sic*] at All Saloons...," *Pueblo Daily Chieftain*, January 24, 1873, 1; "Goldman Received Today a Large Lot of Imported 'Bass' Ale...," *Daily Register* (Central City), February 12, 1873, 3; "Anheuser & Co's St. Louis Beer, in Pints and Quarts, at Sporberg's Centennial Store...," *Colorado Miner* (Georgetown), August 12, 1876, 3; Budweiser advertisement, *Denver Daily Tribune*, October 12, 1878, 1; Budweiser advertisement, *Denver Daily Times*, May 9, 1879, 2; Stanley Baron, *Brewed in America: A History of Beer and Ale in the United States* (Little, Brown, 1962), 257–73; Noel, *City and the Saloon*, 80–81; West, "Dry Crusade," 29. A photo of Seventeenth Street in downtown Denver in 1890 by Rose and Hopkins clearly shows a "Jos. Schlitz Brewing Co." saloon situated prominently on the corner (Denver Public Library Western History Collection, H-583).

57. Coel, Barker, and Gilleland, *Tivoli*; Benson, "Tivoli."
58. Roger V. Clements, "British Investment in the Trans-Mississippi West, 1870–1914: Its Encouragement, and the Metal Mining Interests," *Pacific Historical Review* 29, no. 1 (February 1960): 35–50; Rodman W. Paul with Elliott West, *Mining Frontiers of the Far West, 1848–1880* (University of New Mexico Press, 2001), 111.
59. Roger V. Clements, "British-Controlled Enterprise in the West between 1870 and 1900, and Some Agrarian Reactions," *Agricultural History* 27, no. 4 (October 1953): 132–41; Roger V. Clements, "The Farmers' Attitude Toward British Investment in American Industry," *Journal of Economic History* 15, no. 2 (June 1955): 151–59; Roger V. Clements, "British Investment and American Legislative Restrictions in the Trans-Mississippi West, 1880–1900," *Mississippi Valley Historical Review* 42, no. 2 (September 1955): 207–28.
60. "American Breweries," *The Statist* 23 (June 1, 1889): 635–36; "Two New Brewery Companies," *The Statist* 23 (June 29, 1889): 748–49; "American Brewery Developments," *The Statist* 24 (September 28, 1889): 355–56; Amy Mittelman, *Brewing Battles: A History of American Beer* (Algora Publishing, 2008), 64–65. See also the articles by Roger V. Clements in the previous note for a more comprehensive overview of British investment in the United States in the late nineteenth century and early twentieth century.
61. "Big Institution," 6 (for example); "Adolph Coor's [*sic*] Beer" advertisement, *Wet Mountain Tribune* (Westcliffe, CO), December 29, 1906, 4; "San Juan Brewery" advertisement, *San Juan Prospector* (Del Norte, CO), December 21, 1907, 4. The "Big Institution" article about Zang's appeared in multiple papers around the same time and seems to have been a form of advertising by the brewery, giving it a platform to respond to criticisms about its recent purchase by a British concern as well as reports of its strong-arm tactics with saloonkeepers (see Noel, *City and the Saloon*, 80) by emphasizing its contribution to the local economy.
62. Kostka, *Pre-Prohibition History*, 19; Baron, *Brewed in America*, 250; Noel, *City and the Saloon*, 81; West, "Dry Crusade," 25–28. Kostka puts the number of breweries higher (twenty-seven by the end of 1878), but his reliance on the *Colorado Transcript* newspaper for most of his information, and the weight of concurrence among other sources, makes it seem likely that his numbers are inflated in this case.
63. This is a crude calculation that divides brewery output in 1878 by the total population in 1880. The range reflects the assumption that a quarter or less of the state's total output was consumed out of state in the late 1870s, since the large Denver breweries that shipped as much as half of their product out of the territory were much more likely to do so than smaller local breweries. As with other estimates, it includes every man, woman, and child in the state and thus dramatically underestimates the volume consumed by those who actually drank beer.
64. Colorado statistics from the *Denver Post*, February 2, 1911, 1, via West, "Dry Crusade," 27; national statistics from "Feed Bills Are Large," *Carbonate Chronicle* (Leadville), June 24, 1912, 8. The article on national consumption habits was reprinted in numerous Colorado newspapers around the same time.

SECOND ROUND

65. Dick Kreck, "High, Dry Times as Prohibition Era Sobered Denver," *Denver Post*, July 3, 2009.
66. Horace Greeley, *New York Tribune*, June 12, 1859.
67. William Byers, *Rocky Mountain News*, February 3, 1875, 3.
68. Royal Melendy, "The Saloon in Chicago," *American Journal of Sociology* 6 (November 1900): 289–306.
69. Noel, *City and the Saloon*, 73.
70. L.C. Paddock, "Insurrection in Colorado during the Years 1913–1914," *Cheyenne County News*, June 25, 1914.
71. Paddock, "Insurrection in Colorado."
72. Daniel Okrent, *Last Call: The Rise and Fall of Prohibition* (Scribner, 2011), 25–26; for beer consumption statistics, see Noel, *City and the Saloon*, 250.
73. Noel, *City and the Saloon*, 111; *Aspen Weekly Times*, October 13, 1906, 1.
74. *Fort Collins Courier* 10, no. 43 (April 5, 1888): 1.
75. *Leadville Herald Democrat*, October 3, 1914, 3.
76. "Devilish Demolition," *Aspen Daily Chronicle*, July 7, 1888.
77. "Alcohol and Pneumonia," *Rifle Reveille*, March 17, 1916.
78. "W.C.T.U. Notes Our Nation's Greatest Crisis," *Routt County Sentinel*, January 19, 1913.
79. Noel, *City and the Saloon*, 73.
80. Carl Abbott, Stephen J. Leonard, and Thomas J. Noel, *Colorado: A History of the Centennial State*, 5th ed. (University Press of Colorado, 2013), 256.
81. Kreck, "High, Dry Times."
82. "State and General," *Salida Record*, March 17, 1916.
83. "Moonshine Brewer Held to Grand Jury," *Steamboat Pilot*, May 23, 1917, 1.
84. Annie Nelson and Hadiya Evans, "Science Lounging: Speakeasies and Prohibition," Denver Public Library (blog), November 21, 2014, history.denverlibrary.org/news/science-lounging-speakeasies-and-prohibition.
85. Okrent, *Last Call*, 250–51.
86. *Lima News*, March 31, 1929; James A. Maxwell, "'To the Malt, Add Hops': A Memoir of the Home-Brew Era," *Chicago* 1, no. 2 (1954): 26–29.
87. Kreck, "High, Dry Times."
88. August A. Busch Jr., "As Beer Draws Near," *American Legion Monthly* 14 (January 1933): 20, quoted in Maureen Ogle, *Ambitious Brew: The Story of American Beer* (Harcourt, 2006), 184.
89. Betty L. Alt and Sandra K. Wells, *Mountain Mafia: Organized Crime in the Rockies* (Dog Ear Publishing, 2008), 7–21.
90. Kreck, "High, Dry Times."
91. Alt and Wells, *Mountain Mafia*, 15–28.
92. Dick Kreck, *Smaldone: The Untold Story of an American Crime Family* (Fulcrum Publishing, 2016), 8–13.
93. Fay Warrington and Leslie N. Taullie, eds., *Colorado State Patrol, 1935–1995* (self-published, 1995), 37–38.

94. Warrington and Taullie, *Colorado State Patrol*, 36–42.
95. "The Police Seize Trunks in Hunt for Carlino," *Denver Post*, March 20, 1931, 10.
96. Robert Alan Goldberg, *Hooded Empire: The Ku Klux Klan in Colorado* (University of Illinois Press, 1982), 66.
97. David M. Ralston to William Sweet, September 29, 1923, Box 6, Records of the Office of the Governor, quoted in Goldberg, *Hooded Empire*, 66.
98. See Goldberg, *Hooded Empire*, 59–67.
99. *Pueblo Chieftain*, February 25, 1924.
100. *Walsenburg World*, January 20, 1924.
101. *Denver Express*, January 3, 1922.
102. Goldberg, *Hooded Empire*, 19; Merriam-Webster Dictionary, "scofflaw."
103. Kreck, "High, Dry Times."
104. *Denver Post*, April 27, 1923.
105. See Betty Jo Brenner, "The Colorado Women of the Ku Klux Klan," *Colorado Magazine Online* (April 14, 2021), historycolorado.org/story/2021/04/14/colorado-women-ku-klux-klan.
106. See Goldberg, *Hooded Empire*, 15–35.
107. *Denver Post*, August 8, 1924.
108. Goldberg, *Hooded Empire*, 32.
109. See Goldberg, *Hooded Empire*, 15–35.
110. "Colorado Holds Out Hope for Beer by End of Week: Local Option Clause Still Threatens to Hold Up Measure Providing for Sale," *Rocky Mountain News*, April 4, 1933, 1.
111. Robert L. Chase, "Denver Gets No Midnight Beer," *Rocky Mountain News*, April 6, 1933, 1, 4; Robert L. Chase, "Denver Greets Beer in Orderly Fashion," *Rocky Mountain News*, April 8, 1933, 1; Gene Cervi, "Beer Becomes Legal Here but City Sleeps Thru It," *Rocky Mountain News*, April 7, 1933, 11.
112. United Press, "Beer Will Block Repeal, Say Prohibition Leaders," *Rocky Mountain News*, April 3, 1933, 2; Chase, "Denver Gets No Midnight Beer," 1, 4.
113. Chase, "Denver Gets Beer Back in Orderly Fashion," 1, 3.
114. Flora G. Orr, "Women Wets Invite Drys to Co-Operate," *Rocky Mountain News*, April 6, 1933, 4.
115. Nathan Michael Conzine, "Right at Home: Freedom and Domesticity in the Language and Imagery of Beer Advertising, 1933–1960," *Journal of Social History* (Summer 2010): 843–66; Ogle, *Ambitious Brew*, 204–16.
116. Conzine, "Right at Home," 848–50.
117. Ogle, *Ambitious Brew*, 206, 208, 213–15.

THIRD ROUND

118. Portions of this chapter were first published in *Journal of the West* 55, no. 2 (Spring 2016). Used with permission.

119. "Coors' Golden Brewery Employing 125 Golden Men to Make Real Beer," *Colorado Transcript* (Golden), April 6, 1933, 1; Robert L. Chase, "Revival of State Industry Marks Legal Beer's Return," *Rocky Mountain News*, April 7, 1933, 1.
120. Dan Baum, *Citizen Coors: An American Dynasty* (William Morrow, 2000), 22–25. Saying, "We want people to drink more of our beer, not less," Adolph Jr. and his son Bill had developed a beer with only 3.6 percent alcohol by volume and slightly fewer calories than the regular Coors recipe (4.5 percent), which they sold as Coors Light Beer until wartime rationing forced them to discontinue the product despite strong sales.
121. Baum, *Citizen Coors*, 150; Ogle, *Ambitious Brew*, 273.
122. Grace Lichtenstein, "Sold Only in the West, Coors Beer Is Smuggled to the East. Henry Kissinger Drinks It. So Does Paul Newman, Though He Would Abhor the Coors Family's Politics," *New York Times*, December 28, 1975.
123. Baum, *Citizen Coors*, 48. Baum cites the year 1957 as one in which Coors was atop the sales charts throughout the West.
124. Baum, *Citizen Coors*, 48–52; Beth Mende Conny, *Coors, a Catalyst for Change: The Pioneering of the Aluminum Can* (Adolph Coors Company, 1990).
125. Lichtenstein, "Sold Only in the West"; "Coors Ranks 9th in National Beer Sales," *Rocky Mountain News*, July 12, 1964, 62; "Coors Is 7th largest Beer Seller in U.S.," *Rocky Mountain News*, August 2, 1968, 95; Warren Lowe, "Coors Beer Sales Climb to Record; 5th Largest," *Rocky Mountain News*, January 23, 1969, 61; "Coors 'Nails Down' 5th Largest," *Denver Post*, January 20, 1970, 27; "Coors Bolsters No. 4 Stand in Beer Brewing," *Denver Post*, February 16, 1975, 1E; "Coors, More than Just a Brewer," *Denver Post*, November 11, 1974, 29; Baum, *Citizen Coors*, 96.
126. Ogle, *Ambitious Brew*, 273–74; John Porter, *All About Beer* (Doubleday and Company, 1975), 43; "The Beer that Won the West," *TIME* (February 11, 1974); historic inflation calculation from Bureau of Labor Statistics CPI Inflation Calculator, converting 1975 dollars to 2019 value.
127. This wording comes from an early Coors Brewing Company television advertisement from the 1950s. Courtesy of the Coors Archive, Golden, Colorado.
128. Conny, *Coors*, 10; "Coors Initiates Aluminum Cans," *Denver Post*, January 14, 1959, 42; Al Nakkula, "First Aluminum Beer Can Produced by Adolph Coors Co. of Golden," *Rocky Mountain News*, January 14, 1959, 32; Sam Bock, "Crafting the Can: What the Aluminum Beer Can Teaches Us About the Twenty-First-Century West," *Journal of the West* 55, no. 2 (Spring 2016): 42–46.
129. "Youths Leave Beer Can Hangover," *Douglas County News*, September 24, 1964; Clarissa W. Fletcher, "Letter to the Editor," *Steamboat Pilot*, May 9, 1963; Gordon G. Gauss, "Roadside Litter Costs $500,000," *Rocky Mountain News*, January 26, 1969, 5; cited in Bock, "Crafting the Can," 45.
130. John A. Kouwenhoven, *The Beer Can by the Highway: Essays on What's American about America* (Johns Hopkins University Press, 1988).
131. Robert L. Perkin, "Aluminum Can Could Ease Litter Problem," *Rocky Mountain News*, June 18, 1955.

132. Nakkula, "First Aluminum Beer Can," 32.
133. Morton L. Margolin, "Coors Wages War on Litter," *Rocky Mountain News*, February 21, 1965, 65.
134. "Coors Launches Cash for Cans Program," *Golden Transcript*, January 15, 1970, 6, 8; "Coors Opens Cash for Cans Project," *Rocky Mountain News*, January 16, 1970, 89; "Coors Will Buy Its Used Glass Bottles to Reduce Litter," *Denver Post*, January 7, 1971, 16; "Colorado Leads the Nation in Aluminum Can Recycling," *Rocky Mountain News*, August 15, 1985, 36; Bock, "Crafting the Can," 45–46; Conny, *Coors*, 92–95.
135. U.S. Census Bureau, "Population of the United States: 1970 and 1960," retrieved from census.gov/library/publications/1971/dec/pc-v1.html.
136. For more on racial discrimination and the GI Bill, see Ira Katznelson, *When Affirmative Action Was White: An Untold History of Racial Inequality in Twentieth-Century America* (W.W. Norton, 2005), 140.
137. Abbott, Leonard, and Noel, *Colorado*, 319–22; Carl Ubbelohde, Maxine Benson, and Duane A. Smith, *A Colorado History*, 9th ed. (WestWinds Press, 2006), 333–36; Jason L. Hanson and Julie Peterson, "Zoom In: The Centennial State in 100 Objects," exhibition at the History Colorado Center, opened in 2017.
138. Carl Abbott, *Colorado: A History of the Centennial State* (University Press of Colorado, 1976), 233–35; Abbott, Leonard, and Noel, *Colorado*, 325; U.S. Census Bureau statistics.
139. Ubbelohde, Benson, and Smith, *Colorado History*, 348.
140. Ubbelohde, Benson, and Smith, *Colorado History*, 348; Silvia Pettem, "Boulder Population Nearly Doubled in the 1950s," *Daily Camera* (Boulder), January 12, 2010; Laura Snider, "Extensive Survey of Post-WWII Architecture Examines Impact of Boulder Subdivisions," *Daily Camera* (Boulder), September 25, 2010.
141. Jay R. Brooks, "In This Friendly, Freedom-Loving Land of Ours—Beer Belongs…Enjoy It!" *All About Beer Magazine* 30 no. 5 (November 1, 2009); Nathan Michael Corzine, "Right at Home: Freedom and Domesticity in the Language and Imagery of Beer Advertising, 1933–1960," *Journal of Social History* 43, no. 4 (Summer 2010): 856.
142. Ogle, *Ambitious Brew*, 208.
143. Kostka, *Pre-Prohibition History*, 33.
144. "Brewery Workers Strike for Union Recognition," *Colorado Transcript* (Golden), March 16, 1916; Alan Gersten, "Coors Bearish on the Beer Industry," *Rocky Mountain News*, October 10, 1978, 64.
145. Baum, *Citizen Coors*, 17.
146. "Giant Rips Coors 'Extremism': Birch Society Reprint Cited," *Rocky Mountain News*, May 15, 1962.
147. Baum, *Citizen Coors*, 88–92.
148. Quoted in Baum, *Citizen Coors*, 92.
149. Allyson P. Brantley, "'Givin' Up Our Beer for Sweeter Wine': The Boycott of Coors Beer, Interracial Coalition-Building, and the Making of Business Conservatism, 1957–1987," PhD diss., Department of History, Yale University, 64.
150. Brantley, "Givin' Up Our Beer," 64–75.

151. B. Erin Cole and Allyson Brantley, "The Coors Boycott: When a Beer Can Signaled Your Politics," Colorado Public Radio, October 3, 2014.
152. B. Erin Cole, "A Brewing Controversy: The Coors Boycott, 1967–1987," *Journal of the West* 55, no. 2 (Spring 2016): 32–41; Allyson P. Brantley, *Brewing a Boycott: How a Grassroots Coalition Fought Coors and Remade American Consumer Activism* (University of North Carolina Press, 2022). Brantley's work in its entirety is an exceptionally informative source on the history of the boycott; she discusses Coors's corporate citizenship on page 178, among other places.
153. Bill Coors in 2004 at Coors Field Days in Center, Colorado, quoted by Steve Rockhold, MillerCoors director of brewing materials, e-mail and slide deck sent to the authors on November 1, 2013.
154. *Colorado Transcript* (Golden), April 13, 1898. This ad appeared in the paper for several successive weeks.
155. "Coors Moravian Malting Barley," pamphlet, Adolph Coors Company, circa 1954; Steve Rockhold, to the authors, November 1, 2013.
156. "The Coors Story," *Rocky Mountain News*, July 4, 1948, A-1, A-2; "Brewery Buys Ranch to Develop Malt Barley," *Rocky Mountain News*, February 16, 1949; "San Luis Farm Now Base for Barley Experiments," *Denver Post*, August 14, 1949, 1, 3C; Warren Lowe, "Coors' New Warehouse Is Formally Opened Here," *Rocky Mountain News*, November 18, 1949, 26; *Steamboat Pilot*, October 13, 1949, 6; "New Storage Provided for Coors Barley Program," *Record-Journal of Douglas County* (Castle Rock), May 2, 1952, 2; "Coors Finished Unique Brewery Malthouse," *Douglas County News* (Castle Rock), July 11, 1957, 16; "Coors to Build Barley Facility," *Rocky Mountain News* via Associated Press, May 14, 1970, 6; Morton L. Margolin, "Coors Is Building Barley Storage Unit," *Rocky Mountain News*, December 29, 1971, 77; Michael A. Boland and Gary W. Brester, "Vertical Integration in the Malting Barley Industry: A 'Silver Bullet' for Coors?" *Review of Agricultural Economics* 28, no. 2 (2006): 280; Steve Rockhold, to the authors, November 1, 2013.
157. "Coors Moravian Malting Barley," pamphlet.
158. Margolin, "Coors Is Building Barley Storage Unit," 77.
159. Boland and Brester, "Vertical Integration in the Malting Barley Industry," 280; Tom Rees, "San Luis Valley Farmers Answer Coors," *Rocky Mountain News*, December 14, 1972; Baum, *Citizen Coors*, 110+; Steve Rockhold, "Sourcing Brewing Materials for High Quality Beer," (slide deck), 2008. Coors's insistence on increasingly high-quality barley from its growers is long-standing, as Bill Coors reminded San Luis Valley growers in his 1972 letter. Coors now runs a research facility near Burley, Idaho, in addition to the farm in Center, Colorado. Rockhold includes copies of recent contracts.
160. Boland and Brester, "Vertical Integration in the Malting Barley Industry," 280–81; Harry Schumacher, "Big Beer: Light in the Storm," *New Brewer* (May/June 2013): 86. Boland and Brester report that for protein levels above 10.5 percent, each percentage point results in a reduction of 0.5 to 0.6 percent of beer produced. To illustrate, they suggest that 22,222 pounds of typical Coors barley should produce 750 barrels of beer, but using a protein content above 10.5

percent might produce only 720 barrels. Schumacher reports for the Brewers Association that MillerCoors's combined shipments across all brands totaled 59.625 million barrels in 2011 and 58.95 million in 2012.

161. Rees, "San Luis Valley Farmers Answer Coors," 10; Baum, *Citizen Coors*, 110.
162. Steve Rockhold, to the authors, November 1, 2013. As of 2013, the San Luis Valley was the second-largest producer of Coors barley, with 151 growers cultivating roughly 6.75 million bushels of barley on 45,000 acres. That year, the valley, combined with the fields under contract in northern Colorado, accounted for 16 percent of all the barley needed by the company (now called MillerCoors since a 2008 merger). Of the barley used by MillerCoors, 16 percent comes from Colorado, 11 percent from Wyoming, 31 percent from Idaho, and 24 percent from Montana. The rest is supplied by third-party growers and maltsters.
163. See, for example, the *Creede Candle*, December 8, 1906.
164. George J. Fix, "Explorations in Pre-Prohibition American Lagers," *Brewing Techniques* (May/June 1994); Baum, *Citizen Coors*, 19.
165. Adolph Coors Jr. to Bill Moomey, quoted in Baum, *Citizen Coors*, 32–33.
166. Cole, "Brewing Controversy," 32–41; Brantley, "Givin' Up Our Beer," 17.
167. Keith Villa, communication with the authors, Arvada, Colorado, June 11, 2019.
168. Kostka, *Pre-Prohibition History*, 33; Dave Johnson, communication with the authors, Golden, Colorado, April 21, 2023.

FOURTH ROUND

169. Portions of this chapter were first published in *Journal of the West* 55, no. 2 (Spring 2016). Used with permission.
170. Tom Acitelli, *The Audacity of Hops: The History of America's Craft Beer Revolution* (Chicago Review Press, 2013), 179; interview with Brian Callahan of New Belgium Brewery by Sam Bock, April 23, 2014.
171. For more on Coors's role in promoting Colorado craft beer, see Jonathan Shikes, *Denver Beer: A History of Mile High Brewing* (The History Press, 2020), 32.
172. Weston La Barre, "Native American Beers," *American Anthropologist* 40, no. 2 (1938): 224–34; Patrick J. Abbott, "American Indian and Alaska Native Aboriginal Use of Alcohol in the United States," *American Indian and Alaska Native Mental Health Research* 7, no. 2 (1996): 1–13; Stanley Baron, *Brewed in America: A History of Beer and Ale in the United States* (Little, Brown, and Company, 1962), 3–17; Schell, "Women + Beer."
173. Baron, *Brewed in America*, 95–97; George Washington, "To Make Small Beer," in Notebook as a Virginia Colonel, 1757, George Washington Papers, Series IV, New York Public Library.
174. West, "Beer," citing William Clark's journal entry for October 21, 1805; Arnold, *Eating on the Santa Fe Trail*, 67–68.
175. Charlie Papazian, *The Complete Joy of Homebrewing* (Avon Books, 1984), 2. Before it was published as a book, Papazian circulated his manual as a pamphlet for sale to students in his homebrewing classes and to other homebrewers. This version

of the story has been persistent. Maureen Ogle, one of today's leading historians of the U.S. brewing industry, is among those who have repeated it more recently, noting in *Ambitious Brew*, that homebrewing was illegal "thanks to an accidental bit of poor wording written into repeal laws in the 1930s" (277).

176. Federal Revenue Act of 1918, sec 611; Internal Revenue Code of 1939, sec 3030.

177. Henry C. Stockwell Jr. to Senator Al Ulman, April 11, 1977, recorded in *Miscellaneous Tax Bills I*, "HR 2028: To Authorize the Home Production of Beer and Wine," Hearing Before the Subcommittee on Taxation and Debt Management Generally of the Committee on Finance, U.S. Senate (June 19, 1978), 113.

178. Statement of Alan Cranston, *Congressional Record—Senate*, June 12, 1978, 17136; Acitelli, *Audacity of Hops*, 58–59.

179. PL 95-458, October 14, 1978; Michael McCullough, Joshua Berning, and Jason L. Hanson, "Learning by Brewing: Homebrewing Legalization and the Brewing Industry," *Contemporary Economic Policy* (2018): 1–15, doi:10.1111/coep.12394.

180. Colorado Revised Statute 12-47-106, Colorado liquor code. After speaking with researchers at the Colorado Supreme Court library, searching local press, and interviewing others involved with the decision to sponsor the amendment that legalized homebrewing in Colorado, it's our judgment that state legislators weren't hearing an upwelling of desire from the state's homebrewing community to sanction their hobby and so weren't under pressure to make it a legislative priority.

181. Portions of the text in this chapter first appeared in Jason L. Hanson, Michael McCullough, and Joshua Berning, "New West, Brew West: Home Brewing an Industry in the West," *Journal of the West* 55, no. 2 (Spring 2016): 52–62.

182. Charlie Papazian, interview with Jason L. Hanson, Boulder, Colorado, November 13, 2013.

183. For more on political and social transformations in the New West, see Jeff Roche, ed., *The Political Culture of the New West* (University Press of Kansas, 2008); William R. Travis, *New Geographies of the American West: Land Use and the Changing Patterns of Place* (Island Press, 2007); William Riebsame, Hannah Gosnell, and David Theobald, eds., *Atlas of the New West: Portrait of a Changing Region* (W.W. Norton & Company, 1997).

184. Ogle, *Ambitious Brew*, 268–70, 277 ("Dope of the Depression" article quoted on 277).

185. Acitelli, *Audacity of Hops*, 3–11, 35–34, 69; Ogle, *Ambitious Brew*, 258–65.

186. For more on the New West and some of its contours, see Riebsame, Gosnell, and Theobald, *Atlas of the New West*, and Travis, *New Geographies of the American West*.

187. For more on this transformation, see Annie Gilbert Coleman, *Ski Style: Sport and Culture in the Rockies* (University Press of Kansas, 2004), and William Philpott, *Vacationland: Tourism and Environment in the Colorado High Country* (University of Washington Press, 2013).

188. Much of this biography is drawn from a presentation by Charlie Papazian, "What's Brewing in My Kitchen?," at the History Colorado Center, Denver,

November 25, 2019; see also Matthew Shaer, "The Schoolteacher Who Sparked America's Craft Brew Revolution," *Smithsonian Magazine* (June 2020): 34–45; Acitelli, *Audacity of Hops*, 56; Ogle, *Ambitious Brew*, 280; Charlie Papazian, interview with Jason L. Hanson, Boulder, Colorado, November 13, 2013.

189. Charlie Papazian, interview with Jason L. Hanson, Boulder, Colorado, November 13, 2013.

190. Acitelli, *Audacity of Hops*, 78; Ogle, *Ambitious Brew*, 305; Charlie Papazian, "On Growth, Support, and the American Homebrewer's Association," *Zymurgy* (1980): 2; Stan Hieronymus, "Zymurgy: AHA at the Beginning," *Zymurgy* (2003): 7.

191. Papazian, "On Growth, Support, and the American Homebrewer's Association"; Alan Tobey, "The Case for Local Beer," *Zymurgy* (1983): 3.

192. Charlie Papazian, interview with the authors, Boulder, Colorado, August 8, 2014; Sam Bock, "How 'Beer and Steer' Parties Put Colorado at the Center of the Craft Beer World," Colorado Public Radio, October 1, 2014, CPR.org; Ogle, *Ambitious Brew*, 320; Charles Matzen was listed as the "feast services coordinator for the annual Beer and Steer" in the spring 1979 edition of *Zymurgy*. See *Zymurgy* 2, no. 1, 3. The annual event lasted into the 1990s.

193. *Zymurgy* 2, no. 1 (Spring 1979): 3.

194. Charlie Papazian and Charles Matzen, "Beer & Steer," *Zymurgy* 2, no. 1 (Spring 1979): 1.

195. Acitelli, *Audacity of Hops*, 60; Hieronymus, "Zymurgy"; Emil Dimantchev, "Overview Section: Recreation: Nature Based Recreation in the Rockies: The New Value of the Region's Resources," *Colorado College State of the Rockies Report Card* (Colorado College, 2011). See Appendix A.

196. Charlie Papazian, "Traveling with Homebrew," *Zymurgy* (1979): 11–12.

197. Papazian, "Traveling with Homebrew," 11.

198. Acitelli, *Audacity of Hops*, 92; Ogle, *Ambitious Brew*, 319.

199. Hieronymus, "Zymurgy." The first GABF was actually just a small part of the AHA's fourth annual homebrew competition, although it quickly grew to become the AHA's premier event.

200. Acitelli, *Audacity of Hops*, 73.

201. Acitelli, *Audacity of Hops*; Ogle, *Ambitious Brew*, 321; Roger Fillion, "Small-Batch Craft Brewer Taps Coors for Tips on Getting Started," *Rocky Mountain News*, May 23, 2008.

202. Jesse O'Brien, "The Beginnings of Durango's First Brewpub," *Durango Magazine* (August 30, 2018).

203. Acitelli, *Audacity of Hops*, 210.

204. Kimberly Meyer, "Special Report: Brewing up a Storm, Brew Pubs to Tap Area Market," *Rocky Mountain News*, April 5, 1988.

205. Shikes, *Denver Beer*, 63–72. Shikes's book is a go-to reference for Denver brewing history, particularly in the craft era.

206. Shikes, *Denver Beer*, 73–80.

207. Dr. Keith Villa, interview with Sam Bock, Arvada, Colorado, June 12, 2019.

208. Eric Asimov, "Crisp, Complex and Refreshing," *New York Times*, June 29, 2005; Chad Melis, marketing director for Oskar Blues Brewery, phone interview with Sam Bock, Boulder, Colorado, July 29, 2015.
209. Mike Royko quoted in Ogle, *Ambitious Brew*, 216.
210. Chad Melis, interview with Sam Bock, Boulder, Colorado, July 29, 2015.
211. Chad Melis, interview with Sam Bock, Boulder, Colorado, July 29, 2015.
212. "Lagers and Miners and Barrels, Oh My," interview with Katie Strain, Rocky Mountain PBS, July 27, 2024.

LAST CALL

213. Brewers Association, "State Craft Beer Sales and Production Statistics, 2023," brewersassociation.org/statistics-and-data/state-craft-beer-stats; Brewers Association, "Economic Impact," 2023, brewersassociation.org/statistics-and-data/economic-impact-data/#state-impact.
214. Caitlin Gilbert, David Ovalle, and Hannah Zakhareno, "Alcohol Consumption Surged during the Pandemic—and Deaths Followed," *Washington Post*, July 13, 2023; Catherine Pearson, "Alcohol Might Be Ruining Your Orgasm," *New York Times*, October 23, 2023; Meg Wingerter, "Colorado's Quiet Killer: Alcohol Ends More Lives than Overdoses, but There's Been No Intervention," four-part series, January 4, 2024; Ted Alcorn, "Should Alcoholic Beverages Have Cancer Warning Labels?" *New York Times*, April 9, 2024; Susan Dominus, "Is That Drink Worth It to You?" *New York Times Magazine* (June 15, 2024); Dana G. Smith, "How Much Alcohol Is Too Much for a Driver?" *New York Times*, August 5, 2024; Hannah Docter-Loeb, "Alcohol Played a Part in 2.6 Million Deaths in 2019, WHO Says," *Washington Post*, August 19, 2024.

INDEX

J

K

L

M

N

O

P

R

S

T

U

V

W

Z

ABOUT THE AUTHORS

Sam Bock is History Colorado's director of interpretation and publications and hails from that hub of homebrew, Boulder, Colorado. He was the lead exhibition developer for "Beer Here!: Brewing the New West," a museum tour of Colorado's history with a beer in hand. He's the author of numerous articles about Colorado's hoppy history and conducted his graduate work in history at the University of Colorado–Boulder.

Jason L. Hanson is the chief creative officer at History Colorado. He has written and lectured about brewing history in a variety of publications and venues and coauthored *A Ditch in Time: The City, The West, and Water*. When it comes to beer, he believes in being an aficionado, not a connoisseur—a lover, not a snob.